SAY IT BRAVE:
Wisdom and Faith
for Tough Conversations

*A study for small groups based on
the "Speak Eagle" communication model*

By Heidi Petak, Ph.D.

2nd Edition

Printed in the United States of America

ISBN-13: 978-1981339471
ISBN-10: 1981339477

"The purpose of our tough conversations
is not to change each other
but to deepen our dependence on Christ
so that He can change us both."

-Dr. Heidi Petak

TABLE OF CONTENTS   <ins>PAGE</ins>

SESSION ONE
Introduction

Welcome! For this first session, work through the following material together as a group. After this session, you'll begin reading SESSION TWO for next week.

1. Getting to Know You

Let's spend a few minutes getting to know each other.
Take turns sharing
    a. your name
    b. any personal information you would like to share about yourself
    c. what you hope to gain from this study

2. Group Guidelines

Read through the following group guidelines together:

    a. *Confidential-* Commit to keep confidential what others share in your group.

b. *Bring Your Bible-* Bring your Bible or Bible app so you can look up verses and read the noted references in their Biblical context.

c. *Time-* Be time-conscious. Keep your comments brief so everyone can share.

d. *Be Curious-* We tend to try to "fix" each other's problems. Instead of fixing, be curious, asking good questions to probe deeper into what someone might be feeling or to learn the story behind someone's perspective.

3. A Letter for You

Take turns reading the following letter from the author out loud:

Dear friend,

Do you hate tough conversations? I've hated them all my life- you know, those interactions that require us to reveal our true hearts and risk offending another person. Conversations like revealing your hurt to your mother about her comments, requesting that your neighbors pick up their dog's piles in your yard, or asking a co-worker to respect your privacy. Even more risky is dialogue on hot-button topics like politics, race, and sexuality. After watching friendships dissolve, family members cutting off from each other, and people throwing verbal bombs online at anyone who sits on the other side of the ideological fence, the need to learn to discuss difficult topics in life-giving ways has become dramatically apparent.

But for some of us, heart-revealing conversations feel scary. Maybe that's why we often opt out of them by avoiding, making a snide comment online, or finally exploding when we can't take it anymore. But when we get right down to it, avoiding, "sniding," and exploding are all just ways we protect ourselves. With our fighting words or our silence, we settle for safe and never grapple with our fear. Relational rifts become gaping wounds, and, not knowing how to repair, we resort to avoiding and gossiping and pretending, just to "keep the peace."

Our family suffers. Our churches suffer. Our community suffers. Our hearts suffer.

But God wants more for us. In II Corinthians 3:17, we read, "...where the Spirit of the Lord is, there is liberty." This study is about freedom- finding the faith that fuels the freedom to communicate authentically. Freedom to speak the truth in love. Freedom to walk into and through tough conversations with confidence and faith.

It isn't easy to change our patterns of communicating, so that's why *Say It Brave* is written as a small group study- so you can experience it in community. Surrounded by fellow travelers, you'll benefit from having them encourage you to have patience with yourself, to pray for you, and to give you a safe context in which to practice new ways of communicating. However, if you aren't in a small group, feel free to work through the study on your own.

During the week, spend time reading and answering the questions in the "Let's Talk" sections, writing down your thoughts in the space provided. The sessions aren't divided up into days, so you decide how much you can tackle in one sitting. Then, if and when you meet with your group, discuss what you wrote down in the "Let's Talk" sections, read the Word together and discuss the verses, experience the creative exercise, and pray.

Why a creative exercise, you ask? (I saw you cringe.) Because experiential learning is essential for you to break old habits so that these concepts begin to travel from your head to your heart to your mouth. Experiencing them on a deeper level through creativity will awaken your mind and heart, ignite your self-awareness, and give you courage through Christ to speak life-giving words to those around you.

Through this study, may God so infuse your soul with faith that you will "rise up with wings as eagles," facing each tough conversation with great hope for what He will do in you and through you.

Blessings,
Heidi

4. WORDS FROM THE WORD – Proverbs 15

Look through Proverbs 15 together and find answers to the following questions:

a. What verses in this chapter mention an element of communication, such as speaking or listening? Point them out.

b. In verse 28, we read, "The heart of the righteous ponders how to answer." How do you think our hearts and our mouths are connected?

c. Why do you think God ties communication and righteousness together?

5. **LET'S TALK**

Discuss your answers to the following questions:

a. Are you afraid of tough conversations in which you need to "reveal your true heart and mind and risk offending another person?" Why or why not?

b. If you were to place your fear of tough conversations on a scale, where would you place it? Make an X on the line below.

Not afraid   In the middle   Terrified

c. Some people report having physical symptoms during the moments just before initiating a risky interaction, like a queasy stomach or racing heart. In academic circles, this is called "Communication Apprehension."[1] Check any physical symptoms below that you recall having experienced in the past before initiating a hard conversation.

- ○ queasy stomach
- ○ accelerated heart rate
- ○ dry mouth
- ○ shallow breathing
- ○ shakiness or trembling
- ○ sleeplessness
- ○ sweating
- ○ dizziness or lightheadedness
- ○ chest pain
- ○ numbness or tingling
- ○ confusion
- ○ tightness in my throat

d. Have you ever "opted out" of a difficult conversation? If so, how did you opt out? Did you avoid, offer a snide comment or facial expression, or just explode when you couldn't take it anymore? Which of these strategies do you find yourself doing the most?

6. CREATIVE EXERCISE- "Snapshots"

Think of a posture that represents how you feel about difficult conversations. If you have typically felt anxious, think of how you can use your face, hands, and body to create a snapshot of that anxiety. If you feel indifferent, what does your indifference look like? If you feel confident, what might that confidence look like?

Your group leader will guide you and your fellow group members in using your snapshots to give you a visual picture of the different perspectives in your group. These visual pictures will increase your self-awareness and create a foundation for understanding how your perspective may be affecting your interactions.

7. TALK TO GOD

As you close this group session, pray for...

> *God's Spirit to speak to you through His Word this week to shape your attitude toward tough conversations*
>
> *wisdom to understand the connection between our hearts and our mouths*
>
> *discernment to see and hear the relationship between communication and righteousness*
>
> *courage to face specific risky interactions you may be anticipating this week*
>
> *faith to trust God in the midst of your fear.*

SESSION TWO
Tough Conversations: A Dreaded Necessity

Your heart races. Your hands shake. Your stomach feels like ocean waves, sloshing around, making you feel seasick. Except that you aren't on the sea. You're standing in your kitchen with your phone in your hand, about to call your mother to tell her you're not coming home for Christmas.

Just reading that sentence might make you cringe, imagining the life-long, devastating consequences of throwing a grenade like this to your mother. In fact, you might think it would be much safer to hide the grenade under your bed rather than tell her this news.

Or maybe you're shrugging right now, wondering, "What's the big deal? Tell her the news and she can deal with it. 'Hey Mom, I'm not coming home for Christmas. Deal with it.'" And then she doesn't return your calls for a year and you wonder if perhaps you could have relayed the news a little differently.

Whether we cringe or shrug, we all know tough conversations are a necessary part of life. And, if you're like me, you've experienced one that went badly. Chances are, you've replayed that stressful interaction in your mind, thinking back over what you said and he or she said, wondering what you said that you shouldn't have said, or what you didn't say that you should have said. Toss in falling down the stairs into the school cafeteria in your underwear and you're smack dab in the middle of a nightmare.

You may have been drawn to this study because you've lived the nightmare more than once and even though you dread tough conversations like a root canal, you know you need to have them and want to learn how to do them better. Or, maybe you just want to learn how to do them better with...certain people. When I asked Corey how he felt about tough conversations, he shrugged, "Oh, I'm fine with them. I don't have a problem with talking to anybody about hard stuff." But then he suddenly raised his eyebrows and his voice, pointing his index finger for emphasis, "Unless...unless it's my mother."

Funny how, for so many of us, approaching risky topics with our parents represents the apex of tough conversations. Perhaps it's because we so deeply value our connection with them that their potential rejection of us is tied to some of our greatest fears. However, other individuals, as well, such as bosses, coworkers, spouses, friends, neighbors, relatives, and yes, even fellow church members, may also strike fear in us. Undoubtedly, our experiences sharing difficult information with others in the past have shaped the way we now approach every other potentially risky conversation in our home, workplace, and community.

But we can't stay there. It's time to be courageous. Time to learn new ways of communicating, not from a place of fear, but from a place of faith. Because there's a lot at stake. Our heart connection to the people around us and our influence for Christ in this world depends on us learning how to wisely navigate our most difficult conversations.

In this chapter, we'll first define tough conversations, what they are, when they happen, and where they might take place. Then, we'll investigate the challenge of doing them well, and finally, we'll explore just what in the world they might have to do with faith.

LET'S TALK 1

1. *Do you remember a difficult conversation that went poorly? Describe it.*

2. *With whom do you most fear having a tough conversation right now? Why do you think that might be?*

What, When, Where?

What is a tough conversation? Scholars from the Harvard Negotiation Project say it's "anything you find it hard to talk about."[1] Communication experts at VitalSmarts call them "crucial conversations" and say an ordinary conversation is "crucial" if it affects your life and stakes are high.[2] So, when your neighbor continually lets his dog relieve himself in your yard, your coworker talks behind your back, your significant other has to go, and yes, your mother must be told you won't be coming home for Christmas- all of these situations offer a perfect opportunity for a tough conversation.

Tough conversations feel tough because they are relationally risky, emotionally challenging, mentally taxing, and can be downright exhausting both in preparation and execution. Often they involve the people you love and care about, people who know you well and can read your facial expressions in the dark. You may lose sleep, overeat, undereat, sweat bullets, or even have a near panic attack anticipating them.

When might one happen? Anytime- morning, lunchtime, afternoon, evening, and even the middle of the night. You might have had the pleasure of anticipating the conversation over a few years, or maybe only a few minutes. And because you anticipate it, you might spend time thinking about it and even preparing for it. You may have rehearsed it in your mind or out loud, prayed about it, asked for advice from friends, or even role-played the scenario with a willing party.

And then there are those other opportunities- you know, the ones that appear out of the blue and you don't have any time to anticipate them, such as when you're on the receiving end of a "Can we talk for a minute?" question, or when your boss mentions your great new client and suddenly you realize it's the perfect time to ask for a raise.

Where might one happen? Difficult conversations can happen anywhere you interact with people- home, neighborhood, park, church, school, work, community events and family reunions (definitely family reunions). They may take place one-on-one or in a group setting, on the phone, or virtually through Facetime, Skype, and other virtual means online. And while texting, email, and social media aren't exactly "conversations" in the truest sense of the word, they are still "places" where we often find ourselves revealing our true hearts and minds at the risk of offending others.

Anytime, anywhere, and woven into the very fabric of our lives. Try as we might, we can't get away from them. Situations will inevitably require us to say something risky.

LET'S TALK 2

1. *What topics in your life feel the most risky to address?*

2. *Is there a particular place or area of your life where tough conversations seem to happen more often?*

3. *Think about all of the ways we can communicate today: phone, text, email, Skype, in person, etc. How do you prefer to communicate risky information with others?*

   Why?

4. *How would you prefer for others to communicate difficult information with you?*

Why?

The Risk

Why do hard conversations feel so risky? Because we usually believe we won't be saying what the other person wants to hear. And that's often true. Whether it's a "leaving" conversation like breaking up with a girlfriend or boyfriend, an "I'm frustrated" conversation with a coworker, or a "concerned" conversation with a loved one who isn't making wise decisions, we run the risk of infuriating the other person and suffering from his or her rejection and potential verbal, emotional, or even physical wrath.

The very nature of unpredictability is that we can't control it. And when we can't control something, we experience the feeling of being "out of control." While we can spend many hours of our lives trying to predict how other people will respond, they may still surprise us with a grateful smile or a kick in the gut.

If the unpredictability was about not knowing if a *smile* was coming or not, it wouldn't feel quite so risky. It's the potential for the kick in the gut that feels risky. And the kick doesn't have to be physical. Sometimes it's the verbal kick we fear the most. You know the one. It's the assault that leads to feeling ashamed for having brought up the topic in the first place. And if that happens repetitively, you might eventually run from tough conversations like the bubonic plague. Understandably.

Shame researcher Brene' Brown writes that she feels the most vulnerable when she's "anxious and unsure about how things are going to go," or if she's "having a difficult conversation" or doing something that makes her "uncomfortable" or opens her up "to criticism or judgment."[3] We feel vulnerable when we could be wounded by someone's response, and, tough conversations, by their risky nature, can feel like taking off your bullet-proof vest and opening yourself up to the possibility of being shot through the heart.

WORDS FROM THE WORD
Read Mark 4:35-41

Jesus had a lot to say about fear when He walked on this earth. Put yourself for a moment on the boat with the disciples in the middle of a storm. The waves are crashing over you and you're bailing out water as fast as you can. You're soaked through and panicking, convinced the boat is going to sink and you're going to drown. You frantically wake up Jesus, who is somehow peacefully sleeping on a cushion in the middle of the storm. "Teacher! Don't you care that we're going to die?"

Jesus opens his eyes and looks into your fear-ridden face. He stands, puts His hands out over the roaring waters. He rebukes the wind and commands the sea, "Peace! Be still." The wind stops blowing. The waves stop crashing. The calm is almost tangible. You look at Peter with wide eyes, as if to say, "Did that just really happen?" Then Jesus turns to you, and with great compassion, asks, "Why are you afraid? Have you still no faith?"

Faith. Jesus says it's the antidote to fear.[4] And after seeing Jesus heal a paralyzed man and cast out a demon or two, you would think the disciples would have trusted that the Son of the Almighty God had power over measly storms. But even after Jesus calmed the storm, they were still terrified and whispered to each other, "Who is this that even the wind and the waves obey Him?"

So, if you dread conversational storms, you're in good company. Even the guys who walked with Jesus shivered in their sandals when the wind picked up. But the Lord is full of compassion. He knows our frailty, our fear, our fumbling attempts. In fact, it is precisely these human features that make us lean heavy on Him. In need. In dependence. In faith.

1. *Read the description of "Leviathan" in Job 41. List a few of his most frightening characteristics.*

2. *What other story in the Old Testament might have contributed to the disciples' fear of the sea?*

3. *In your life, what could the storm and the Leviathan represent?*

Faith in What?

So, we know we need to have faith. But faith in what? Faith that we will say the right thing? Well, no, we're fallible humans and we'll undoubtedly make mistakes. Big mistakes. Often. Faith that others will respond how we want them to respond? They'll change just because we told them they should change or accept our tough news without getting upset? We all know that's not faith- that's just our vain imaginations. No, our faith can't rest in other people or in ourselves. Our faith must rest in the One who has the power to change us both.

In his landmark book, *Anatomy of the Soul*, neuroscientist Curt Thompson writes that God can work through our minds, even creating new neural pathways, to transform us.[5] As we come to understand the true character of God, He can transform the way we communicate and respond in tough conversations, founded not on fear, but on trust. Trusting that our God is the Heart-Changer, the Acceptance-Giver, and the Shame-Taker.

God, the Heart-Changer

There is great comfort in knowing I'm not responsible for the decisions and responses of other people. Whether it's my child or my boss, my spouse or my friend, they are responsible for their own choices; only God has the power to change them. Deep, heart-level change is a work of God alone. In Proverbs 21:1, we read, "The king's heart is like channels of water in the hand of the Lord; He turns it wherever He wishes."

This truth doesn't let us off the hook, however, to act like Vivian's father. After Vivian tried to take her own life, her father only said, "That was stupid." No, we are called by God to communicate courageously in ways that point those

20

around us to God. Like Brent. Brent told me this week of a tough conversation he had with his 23-year old daughter, who he had found stumbling around her room after having mixed alcohol, pain meds, and sleeping pills. After he got her medical help, he then asked compassionate questions and they talked openly about ways we all escape from the pain of life. He was faithful to speak the truth in love and then he left the deep work of changing her heart to God.

When we believe we can't change the hearts of others, we are able to ask curious questions and listen without judgment. We don't need to demand that they change or manipulate or shame them into changing; we can love them freely and empathize with them, giving advice when invited, and then rest in the truth that God is writing their stories.

This truth is essential for our perspective because so often we walk into a difficult conversation believing we need to win. The sign of victory for us is when the other people agree with our conclusions and make the choices we want them to make. I know for me, if that happened, I would pat myself on the back for being such a powerful influencer.

But we know that God is about *His* glory, not ours. In fact, He's quite emphatic about it. In Isaiah 42:8, He says, "I am the LORD, that is my name; I will not give My glory to another." Our job is to bring glory to God by facilitating encounters with Him through open sharing, curious questions, and empathetic listening. And if this sparks another to turn to Him, we give Him the credit. However, if we think we're the ones who persuade the heart-change, then we'll strut our stuff. When we believe God is the Heart-Changer then we will be humble and dependent, asking Him to do the ultimate work.

God, the Acceptance-Giver

For many of us, we're afraid of initiating a difficult conversation because it means risking disapproval and rejection. And this is where God, the Acceptance-Giver comes in. No matter how the other person chooses to treat you as a result of the news you share or the boundary you set or the truth you express in love, you will never be abandoned or rejected by your Heavenly Father. You can rest in His ultimate acceptance, love, and approval of you as you have hidden yourself in Christ and His righteousness.

How does that work? Picture Christ as your umbrella. Because He lived a perfect life and shed His blood on the cross as the ultimate sacrifice for your sin, when you step under the umbrella, the covering for your sin that is Jesus, now God looks at you and sees...not you and all your sin and imperfection...but Jesus and all of His perfection and righteousness! Because of Jesus's life, death, and resurrection, we can have a personal relationship with a holy God and bask in His acceptance of us.

A while ago, Marie sent me a text. "Pray for me, Heidi! I'm about to have lunch with my mom!" She had been deeply hurt by her mother's incessant comments about her weight and was finally ready to risk sharing her hurt in a tough conversation. Even if her mother reacted angrily or defensively and again made hurtful comments or even gave her the silent treatment for a month, Marie was able to risk it, knowing that she was ultimately loved and accepted by God. Her stance wasn't self-righteous, but secure; she didn't need to keep silent anymore out of her fear of being rejected.

When God has filled our hearts with His unconditional, forever love, we are able to risk speaking the truth. The significance of God being our Acceptance-Giver cannot be underestimated in terms of what it means for the way we communicate.

God, the Shame-Taker

Our experience of God's acceptance also brings with it another gift- that of freedom from shame. Our fear of shame can be a deadly fuel that drives us to flip our shame around and shame others instead. And so we manipulate, attack, and demoralize others to protect ourselves from the suffocating feeling of shame. But Jesus shows us another way, a humbled, surrendered way that leads to freedom.

In Francine Rivers' book, *The Last Sin Eater*,[6] she tells the haunting story of a man who lives in isolation, deep in the forest. His only job is to take the sin and shame of the nearby villagers upon himself so that they can live in spiritual freedom. Yet, the villagers still don't live in freedom. They live year after year, decade after decade, generation after generation, in bondage, fear, and shame. It isn't until a man of God arrives and shares the good news of Jesus Christ that the villagers find freedom from their shame. Eventually, even the Sin Eater himself is wrapped up in the grace of God. Jesus is the ultimate "Sin-Eater" because He took our sin upon Himself and died so that we could live free.

Try as you might, you can't absolve yourself of shame on your own. But you don't need to. You need only to confess your imperfections, your mistakes, your sin, and let God wrap you up in His grace, His shame-taking grace. "If we confess our sins, He is faithful and righteous to forgive us our sins and to cleanse us from all unrighteousness" (I John 1:9).

For Jesus, surely the mockery, the abandonment of his friends, the heavy weight of our sin, and the utter degradation of hanging naked on a cross would have been a shameful experience. Yet we read in Hebrews 12:2 that Jesus, "for the

joy set before Him endured the cross, despising the shame..."
In the same way, we are to keep our eyes on the joy set before
us and despise shame, knowing that we have hidden
ourselves in the forgiveness of God and the perfection of Jesus
Christ.

CREATIVE EXERCISE- "A Letter from God" (write now and
then share during your small group time if you wish)

*In the space below and on the next page (or in a journal), write
a letter of reassurance to yourself from God, incorporating
verses you find in Scripture that assure you of these two truths-
how God is the One who changes the hearts of others, the One
who accepts and loves you unconditionally, and the One who
has freed you from shame. (Hint: To find verses, search terms
that relate to power, dominion, control, heart, love, etc.)
Incorporate in your letter from God how He is using these
truths to encourage you to trust Him in tough conversations
that lie ahead. If you feel comfortable, read your letter aloud
during your small group time. Or, have someone else read your
letter aloud.*

A letter to me from God:

Can I Be a Good Communicator Without Faith?

Faith isn't required to be a good communicator. Scads of books line bookstore shelves, like *Difficult Conversations*[7] and *Crucial Conversations*,[8] offering readers help to improve their communication skills. More generally speaking, philanthropists who are able to communicate well can do much good in the world and create beautiful, positive change. Motivating, counseling, encouraging, cheering, teaching, and even admonishing can impact the lives of others for positive, earthly, temporal change.

But, earthly, temporal change is different from spiritual, eternal change. As Henry Blackaby teaches in *Experiencing God*, "God invites you to join Him in His work."[9] God's work, while it often does often bring about good things for people on earth, is much more than that; it's a spiritual work that is concerned with souls and hearts, freedom, abundant life, and eternal destinies.

For Christy, joining God in His work meant curbing her urge to "fix" her friends in her tough conversations, and instead, courageously point her friends to God for His counsel. For Ryan, it meant continuing to pursue a relationship with his young adult, transgender son and ask loving, curious questions to better understand. For Tom, this meant an incredibly tough conversation- confessing his pornography addiction to his wife and committing to seek help and accountability. For Monica, it meant taking a risk in breaking up with her boyfriend who was pressuring her to sleep with him. For Grace, it meant embracing vulnerability and sharing her longing for connection with her daughter instead of making snide comments about their disconnection.

For me, it meant taking the scary step of having very difficult conversations about faith, politics, abortion, gender, sexuality, and race relations with my "nontheist" friend from high school, Kellie, finding ways to remain connected to her on a heart level despite our deep disagreements. And then, to provide opportunities for my conservative friends to connect with Kellie's friends for similar conversations. I marveled as I watched my Christian friends share a meal and respectful conversation with two Buddhist environmentalists, a married lesbian couple, and a woman with a transgender child. Not forsaking the gospel for love, but loving for the sake of the gospel. (*See www.HeartPerceptionProject.com.*[10])

Only by faith can we accept God's invitation to join Him, partnering with Him in the spiritual work He is doing in us and in the people around us. For hard conversations, this means we have to look deeper than the facts or the circumstances to consider what God might be doing to draw us to Himself and free us from fear by teaching us to trust Him in the way we communicate.

What's at Stake?

If we are known as believers, we represent God by the way we communicate. Our ability to speak the truth in love, even to people we don't trust, affects the way others view God. Nothing can be more important.

"I blew it," Jeanne, confessed. "My son slept over at a friend's house Saturday night. He knew I was coming the next morning to pick him up for church, but he overslept. And his friend's parents let him sleep! I marched up to the door in my Sunday best and banged until they answered it. And then I really let the mother have it. She doesn't share my faith or understand how important church is to me. But then...but then I saw my son's face. He was mortified by my behavior. And actually, I was, too."

Tough conversation. A lot of truth- no love. And while Jeanne's testimony as a believer in Christ is not irreparable, she had shot it through with a verbal 45 caliber pistol. Holes like that are hard to repair.

If we are to be salt and light in the world, we must take our "talk" seriously. There are souls at stake. Communication professor, Quentin Schultze, writes, "...everything we do as disciples is a witness to the world. We truly cannot *not* communicate. Our entire lives speak what we believe and what we love."[11]

People are listening. People are watching. Our ability or inability to speak the truth in love impacts the way others see our God and their desire to know Him. While we may never communicate perfectly this side of heaven, God graciously invites us to partner with Him in the work He is doing to draw us and those around us into relationship with Him.

LET'S TALK 4

Has there been someone in your life who interacted with you in a way that drew you to God? If so, describe how that person communicated.

Scope and Purpose

In the following chapters, you'll first identify your own communication styles in your various relationships and then we'll look a little more deeply at all of our fear-based tendencies to see what drives them and how they might be transformed by greater faith. Finally, we'll explore what it looks like when we tie faith and communication together with life-giving strategies.

Peppered with narrative accounts from three years of informal interviews with countless clients, students, and friends (most names have been changed to protect their identities), you'll be drawn in to explore your own motivations, wrestle with your fears and insecurities, and explore the dynamic characters in the Word of God to see how their faith dramatically changed the way they communicated.

The purpose of this study is to help you grow in your self-awareness of your own choices, to give you a place to explore your best options for communicating in specific tough conversations, and to encourage you to trust the Lord more fully. As you learn to trust Him, it's my hope that your perspective, preparation, and experience of tough conversations will be marked by faith, freeing you to truly speak the truth in love. I believe if we take the very best that professional mediators, counselors and communication experts have to offer and soak it in an unshakable faith in the character of God, our toughest conversations can become some of our deepest and most life-changing interactions.

TALK TO GOD

Pray that you would have...

> the faith to believe He is the One who changes hearts and the One who fully and unconditionally loves and accepts you

> the humility to apologize when you have not represented Him well in your communication

> a commitment to join Him in the spiritual work He is doing in your heart and the hearts of those around you

> and finally, that He would use your communication to draw others to Him.

SESSION THREE
Your Communication Style

Becky heard a battle cry outside her apartment and ran to the open window just in time to see her big, burly, red-headed husband, John, lift his shoe out of the grass in the common area and utter a primal growl. And then she watched him turn in rage to the balcony upstairs where his neighbor, Jeff, was entertaining a date, complete with music and candlelight.

"Hey Jeff! You see this?" he yelled, pointing at his foot. "I just stepped in your dog's pile! And I know it's yours because he's the only dog on this side of the building! I am sick of this! Now, get down here and clean it up!" An unintelligible retort was heard from Jeff. John kept yelling. "No, it can't wait till later!" he shouted, "I'm done with you leaving your dog's mess down here!"

Becky's brown eyes widened from behind the window and she just about swallowed her gum. "Wow. I'm glad I'm not out there," she thought.

The dark-haired, bearded Jeff appeared a few minutes later with a plastic bag. He scowled at John, "Thanks for ruining my date."

Becky slunk back from the window. She was sick of the piles, too, but never would have said something at a time like this. She would have quietly cleaned her shoe and stuffed her anger.

While her husband clearly wasn't worried about whom he ticked off in the apartment complex, she, on the other hand, preferred to use other methods of expression, like telling another neighbor about her frustration. Once, however, in a moment of what she called "sheer brilliance," she did take a picture of a pile and put it on their apartment's online forum, saying she didn't leave her baby's dirty diapers in the common area, so certain people shouldn't leave their dog's business on the grass. However, as brazen as that seemed, she still wouldn't even think of confronting Jeff face-to-face and telling him how infuriated she was by his irresponsibility. That would be too uncomfortable.

But something needed to change. Maybe it was a good thing John had exploded at Jeff. Maybe it would make Jeff think twice before walking away without cleaning up after his dog. "That would be nice," Becky thought.

And then another, not-so-optimistic thought crossed her mind. What if John's yelling actually made it worse? He certainly embarrassed Jeff in front of his date. What if Jeff keyed their car or left dog piles in front of their door? And then what if John retaliated in a more...dramatic way, like kicking Jeff's dog, and then Jeff sued them and they had to sell off their assets to pay the legal fees?

"So what happened?" I asked Becky as we talked on the phone.

"Well, none of that happened, thankfully," she laughed. "I guess my imagination got the best of me. But we have decided to move to a different apartment building. It's just too stressful."

What would YOU do?

John, Becky, and Jeff have each developed very different patterns in the way they communicate with people in certain situations, patterns that undoubtedly carry over to how they express themselves with their family members and at work as well. How about you?

LET'S TALK 1
In what way are you more like Becky, John, or Jeff?

I'm definitely more like Becky. I'm an avoider and a stuffer. Except with my kids. I can be very assertive with my four boys ("Get off the roof, NOW!") but put me in a conversation with an adult with a strong personality and I'm quite content to smile and keep my mouth shut. My friend, Joy, is the adult with the strong personality. She says exactly what she thinks and rather enjoys conflict. I don't understand her, but I still like her.

Even Joy, though, explained that she communicates a little differently depending on the situation, such as how much authority she believes the another person has. For example, she tends to be very outspoken with her friends but is a little more careful with her boss at work. She also tends to be more direct when she feels like she has some expertise, but is less outspoken if she knows she isn't the expert in the room. You have probably found that you also adapt your communication style to the other person or to the situation.

But even with all these variables, I believe we all still have tendencies in the way we communicate. Born of your upbringing, your personality, and your experiences, your communication style is the way you typically choose to exchange verbal and nonverbal messages with others to meet your goals. Said more plainly, it's how you "speak" to get what you want. In this case, you are considering especially how you "speak" when you face conflict or difficult conversations with particular people in your life. And "speaking" isn't limited to words- it's anything you say or do that communicates a message to another person.

To create a comprehensive picture of how you communicate across your most important relationships, take the following two-part assessment. For each question, you will consider how you communicate in one relationship at a time. For broader categories, such as children, employees, friends, or parents, perhaps choose one person with whom you have a challenging relationship. You'll investigate the way you communicate with your Romance (such as your spouse, boyfriend, or girlfriend), one of your Children, one of your Parents, your Boss, Board Chair or other person or people to whom you report, one of your Co-workers, Employees or subordinates, and a Friend. Two places are left blank for you to write in other relationships you would like to investigate (such as another child, friend, sibling, co-worker, or parent).

Consider each question and write your answer on the line next to that relationship. Choose the answer that corresponds with your strongest inclination, or how you think have most often communicated in the past in that type of relationship.

THE "SPEAK EAGLE" COMMUNICATION STYLE
ASSESSMENT
PART I

1. In the way I have communicated with this person in the past, I have been primarily
    A. agreeable and peaceful
    B. strategic and influential
    C. bold and outspoken

    Romance____ Child____ Parent____ Boss____
    Co-worker____ Employee____ Friend____
    [   ]___ [   ]___

2. When this person has communicated aggressively, I have
    A. kept quiet about what I really think
    B. told someone else what I really think
    C. told him or her directly what I really think

    Romance____ Child____ Parent____ Boss____
    Co-worker____ Employee____ Friend____
    [   ]___ [   ]___

3. When this person has needed to be confronted, I have
    A. talked myself out of doing the confronting
    B. thought of a way to confront indirectly
    C. confronted him or her

    Romance____ Child____ Parent____ Boss____
    Co-worker____ Employee____ Friend____
    [   ]___ [   ]___

4. When I didn't like something this person was doing, I
    A. kept it to myself
    B. expressed my dislike without saying it directly
    C. said I didn't like it

    Romance____   Child____   Parent____   Boss____
    Co-worker____   Employee____   Friend____
    [   ]____   [   ]____

5. When I have sensed there was conflict brewing with this
    person, I
    A. avoided it by pretending everything was okay
    B. made a clever comment about it
    C. addressed it directly

    Romance____   Child____   Parent____   Boss____
    Co-worker____   Employee____   Friend____
    [   ]____   [   ]____

6. When I needed to communicate something difficult with
    this person, I
    A. tried to find a way out of it
    B. procrastinated
    C. said what needed to be said

    Romance____   Child____   Parent____   Boss____
    Co-worker____   Employee____   Friend____
    [   ]____   [   ]____

7. When I have needed to ask for help from this person, I
   A. tried to find another way to get my needs met
   B. dropped a lot of hints
   C. told him or her I needed help

   Romance____   Child____   Parent____   Boss____
   Co-worker____   Employee____   Friend____
   [   ]____ [   ]____

8. When I have been frustrated with this person, I have
   A. shied away from telling him or her
   B. used my face and tone of voice to show how I feel
   C. been direct with him or her about how I feel

   Romance____   Child____   Parent____   Boss____
   Co-worker____   Employee____   Friend____
   [   ]____ [   ]____

9. When I have wanted to resist a decision I didn't agree with, I
   A. talked myself out of resisting
   B. resisted covertly
   C. resisted confidently

   Romance____   Child____   Parent____   Boss____
   Co-worker____   Employee____   Friend____
   [   ]____ [   ]____

10. When this person has hurt my feelings, I
    A. kept it to myself
    B. showed it with my actions
    C. expressed my hurt clearly with my words

    Romance____ Child____ Parent____ Boss____
    Co-worker____ Employee____ Friend____
    [   ]___ [   ]___

11. When I have been concerned about this person's
    behavior, I
    A. stayed quiet about it
    B. told someone else
    C. directly communicated my concern with him or her

    Romance____ Child____ Parent____ Boss____
    Co-worker____ Employee____ Friend____
    [   ]___ [   ]___

Scoring

Now, score your answers, writing down the number of times
you chose A, B, or C for each relationship. Then, write down
the letter you chose most along with the number of times you
chose that answer, such as B7, in the blank after "Letter you
chose most."

Romance   A ____ B ____ C ____
             Letter you chose most: _____

Child   A ____ B ____ C ____
             Letter you chose most: _____

Parent   A ___   B ___   C ___
                 Letter you chose most: ____

Boss   A ___   B ___   C ___
                 Letter you chose most: ____

Co-worker   A ___   B ___   C ___
                 Letter you chose most: ____

Employee   A ___   B ___   C ___
                 Letter you chose most: ____

Friend   A ___   B ___   C ___
                 Letter you chose most: ____

[   ] A ___   B ___   C ___
                 Letter you chose most: ____

[   ] A ___   B ___   C ___
                 Letter you chose most: ____

Each score corresponds to a category along a horizontal axis that measures assertiveness, with the letter A representing the thoughtful/passive communicator, the letter B representing the strategic/passive-aggressive communicator, and the letter C representing the courageous/aggressive communicator.

Now, write your different relationships in the boxes below using abbreviations such as "Ro" for Romance (or the name of your significant other), and "Bo" for Boss (or the name of your boss), etc. Or, you can write the name of the person instead.

If you chose the same category for two or more relationships, place the relationship in which you scored the highest the furthest to the right in the box. For example, if you scored a B7 with your Romance, but a B8 with your Boss, write the abbreviation "Bo" further to the right of "Ro" in the Strategic "B" box below.

ASSERTIVENESS SCALE

A Thoughtful	B Strategic	C Courageous

less
assertive

more
assertive

While this baseline category to measure your assertiveness is informative about the way you prefer to communicate in each of these relationships, there is another key factor that moderates how you communicate within that category. Take Part II of the assessment to find out how this key factor may be affecting your communication choices.

Thoughtfully consider each statement in regards to each of your important relationships. Then, write the corresponding number of the emoji that illustrates the degree to which you think the statement is true in that relationship. Repeat for each relationship.

PART II

1. This person wants to hear what I have to say.

1	2	3	4	5

Romance____ Child____ Parent____ Boss____
Co-worker____ Employee____ Friend____
[   ]____ [   ]____

2. My role or position in this relationship is secure.

1	2	3	4	5

Romance____ Child____ Parent____ Boss____
Co-worker____ Employee____ Friend____
[   ]____ [   ]____

3. This person respects me.

1	2	3	4	5

Romance____ Child____ Parent____ Boss____
Co-worker____ Employee____ Friend____
[   ]____ [   ]____

4. This person sees me as an essential part of this team/relationship.

1   2   3   4   5

Romance____   Child____   Parent____   Boss____
Co-worker____ Employee____   Friend____
[   ]____ [   ]____

5. In making decisions, this person has my best interests in mind.

1   2   3   4   5

Romance____   Child____   Parent____   Boss____
Co-worker____ Employee____   Friend____
[   ]____ [   ]____

6. This person is speaking well of me.

1   2   3   4   5

Romance____   Child____   Parent____   Boss____
Co-worker____ Employee____   Friend____
[   ]____ [   ]____

7. This person values my voice.

1   2   3   4   5

Romance_____ Child_____ Parent_____ Boss_____
Co-worker_____ Employee_____ Friend_____
[   ]_____ [   ]_____

8. This person will make caring choices in situations that affect me.

1   2   3   4   5

Romance_____ Child_____ Parent_____ Boss_____
Co-worker_____ Employee_____ Friend_____
[   ]_____ [   ]_____

9. I will not be rejected in this relationship.

1   2   3   4   5

Romance_____ Child_____ Parent_____ Boss_____
Co-worker_____ Employee_____ Friend_____
[   ]_____ [   ]_____

10. This person will give me grace if I fail or make a mistake.

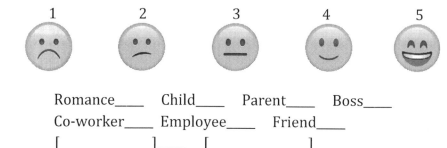

Romance____ Child____ Parent____ Boss____
Co-worker____ Employee____ Friend____
[   ]____ [   ]____

Now, add up the point values of all your answers to find your scores for Part II for each relationship.

TOTAL SCORES:

Romance____ Child____ Parent____ Boss____
Co-worker____ Employee____ Friend____
[   ]____ [   ]____

Part II considers the impact of the Trust Factor. Your score indicates to what degree trust and fear are affecting the way you communicate. Trust, in this assessment, includes 5 necessary elements:

Value- My voice and input are valued.
Respect- This person shows respect for me by words and actions.
Security- I feel secure in this relationship.
Caring- This person cares enough about me to make decisions in my best interest.
Grace- I have the freedom to make mistakes because this person gives me grace.

When these elements of trust are not experienced in the relationship, fear is most likely present. Fear, in this assessment, centers on the fear of experiencing the shame of rejection or failure. When your voice is not valued, you are not respected, you don't feel secure or cared for, and you don't have the freedom to fail, the shame of rejection can feel like it's always waiting right around the corner.

The Trust Factor is a vertical continuum between Fear and Trust, with Fear indicated by a low score and Trust indicated by a high score. Below, write the abbreviation for each relationship to the left of the line near the number that represents your Trust Factor for that relationship.

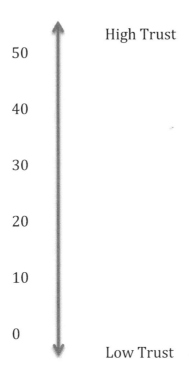

High Trust

50

40

30

20

10

0

Low Trust

WHAT YOUR SCORE MEANS

If you scored between 10-17, you don't experience much trust in this relationship. And with little trust to bank on, your fear is probably high; you do what you have to do to protect yourself and get your needs met. The closer your score to 10, the less you're able to trust, and the more fear may be driving the way you communicate.

If you scored between 18-34, you sometimes experience trust in this relationship, which allows you to occasionally rest and communicate from that place of security. Other times, however, your fear and lack of trust drives you to communicate in defensive ways to protect yourself and get your needs met.

If you scored between 34-50, you experience a significant amount of trust in this relationship and are often able to communicate from that place of rest. The higher your score towards 50, the more secure you feel, laying a foundation for being free to express yourself in life-giving ways.

Once you have your results from Part I and Part II for each relationship (A, B, or C for Part I and a number between 10 and 50 for Part II), you can plot a position on a larger table of communication styles. On the table on the next page, write the abbreviation for each relationship in the place where your two scores meet for that relationship.

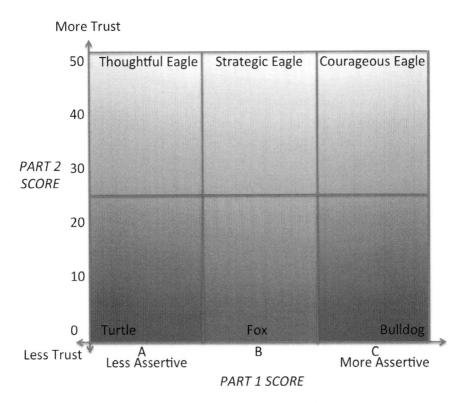

The three communication styles across the top (Thoughtful Eagle, Strategic Eagle, and Courageous Eagle) are three variations on one style which is fueled by high trust in the relationship. We call this style the "Eagle" because this communicator is able to soar with truth and love, especially in difficult conversations. The three communication styles across the bottom are flip-sides of the same coins, but are fueled by fear in the relationship. They are the passive Turtle, the passive-aggressive Fox, and the aggressive Bulldog. We'll be taking a close look at each of these communication styles in the following chapters.

In looking at your relationships on the table, you probably find that you communicate differently depending on how much you trust the person with whom you're interacting, the context or situation, and even particular circumstances. Sometimes you might even flip between styles in the same conversation, especially if the other person responds in a way that encourages your trust or triggers your fear. As we investigate each of the styles in the following chapters, look for patterns in your levels of trust and the way you typically communicate with people closest to you, particular authority levels, genders, ages, or other contributing factors.

Now, let's make the table even more visual with the Speak Eagle Communication Model- a visual diagram of our fear-based and trust-based communication styles.

On the next page, imagine overlaying the six-box chart from the previous page over the animal diagram of the Speak Eagle communication model. Again, write the abbreviation for each of your relationships in the area on the diagram above where your two scores meet. Then, read the descriptions on the following pages of the styles that represent your communication choices in those relationships.

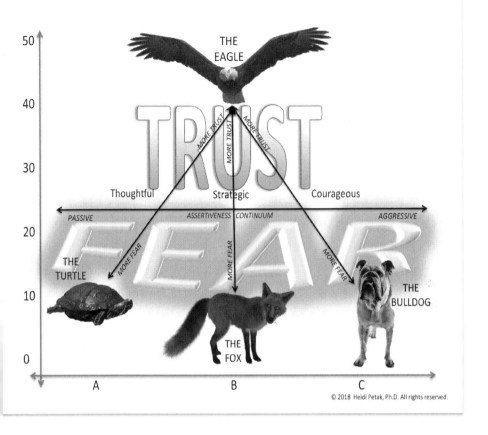

STYLE DESCRIPTIONS

THOUGHTFUL EAGLE: Communicating from a place of trust in this relationship, you are considerate and compassionate, considering the feelings of others first and foremost. You are a good listener and people tend to share their hearts with you easily. If you need to confront, you have learned to courageously speak the truth, but are careful to speak it kindly and use words that still affirm the value of the other person. You are able to be a Thoughtful Eagle because you are not afraid of rejection in this relationship. For you, "brave" means speaking up when it might feel safer to stay silent. When you begin to sense rejection, however, you may default to a Turtle or another fear-based style.

TURTLE: Communicating from a place of fear in this relationship, you are deeply afraid of the shame that envelops you when you sense rejection. You quietly hide what you really think and feel rather than risk a confrontation. Stuff your feelings for too long and you will probably snap. While hiding your true feelings seems like the safest choice in the short run, in the long run, you may sacrifice being truly known. However, as your trust grows, you become less passive, more willing to speak the truth, and more willing to risk being known. It is then that you become a Thoughtful Eagle or another Eagle style.

STRATEGIC EAGLE: Communicating from a place of trust in this relationship, you are able to come out from behind your mask and be vulnerable, sharing honestly what you think and feel. You are wise and discerning, strategizing the best way to speak the truth in love. You are adept at reading another person and know how to guide him or her to self-discovery. Skilled at nuanced communication, you use every tool in your toolbox, including facial expressions and body language to influence others towards their own good and the good of the whole. For you, "brave" means revealing your true heart and mind and asking clearly for what you need, even when it often feels safer to communicate indirectly. However, when you become afraid of revealing weakness, you may default to a Fox or another fear-based style.

FOX: Communicating from a place of fear in this relationship, you are afraid of both rejection and not getting your needs met. You are an expert at communicating what you want without the risk of saying it directly. Because you are so adept at using indirect methods, such as tone of voice, body language, and loaded questions, you are able to dodge implication and resist under the table. While this feels good in the short run, you suffer greatly when you find that your communication style, which often shames others, is destroying trust and sabotaging the relationships you need. However, as your trust grows, you are willing to risk vulnerability, reveal your true heart, and become a Strategic Eagle or another Eagle style.

COURAGEOUS EAGLE: Communicating from a place of trust in this relationship, you are bold, direct, and persuasive. You are able to navigate conflict with confidence in this relationship. In fact, you believe conflict keeps life interesting. You are gifted at speaking the truth and are able to say what others hesitate to say. At the same time, you are able to make the conscious choice to listen well, allow the other person to live freely, and exercise empathy, considering the feelings of others as you interact. Because you build others up and have their best interests in mind, you foster trust and are able to lead courageously. For you, "brave" means loving by letting go when it feels much safer to control. When you begin to feel afraid of losing control, however, you may default to a Bulldog or another fear-based style.

BULLDOG: Communicating from a place of fear in this relationship, you are deeply afraid of losing control. Because of your fear, you are brilliant at using fear to persuade the other person in this relationship to change or to meet your needs. Because you are so vocal with your opinions, others may be intimidated by the way you communicate and might be afraid to tell you the truth. While it feels good in the short run to bark loudly and bite firmly, in the long run you may sacrifice intimacy in this relationship as the other person hides from you. However, as your trust grows, you are able to let go of control and give others freedom as a Courageous Eagle or another Eagle style.

What a beautiful world it would be if we all could be Eagles every moment of every conversation, however, there will undoubtedly be moments in which we feel afraid and default to the flip side of our communication style- even in the same conversation. In fact, you may choose any one of the styles based on what helps you feel the most safe in the moment. You will probably find, however, that you tend towards one style in each relationship. For instance, you may find that when you are afraid, you're a Turtle with your boss, a Fox with your spouse, and a Bulldog with your employees or your children. If your score indicated that you are typically an Eagle in an important relationship, be aware that when you are afraid, you may choose the opposite style. Consider the flip-side of your most frequent Eagle and circle it on the diagram below.

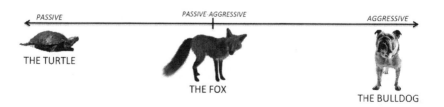

PASSIVE PASSIVE-AGGRESSIVE AGGRESSIVE

THE TURTLE

THE FOX

THE BULLDOG

LET'S TALK 2

1. Look back at the relationships you plotted on the Speak Eagle animal diagram. Do you see any patterns in the way you communicate?

2. If you were to give this quiz to a few people close to you considering the way you communicate with them, how do you think they would answer?

Not a label, a pattern of choices

Your communication style is not a fixed identity marker for a given relationship. So, don't go making yourself a label and sticking it on your forehead. Each style is merely patterns of choices we have made in the past in the way we communicate, based on our level of trust. And, as you have seen, you often make different choices depending on the person and the situation. If you make the same fearful choices consistently over many years in the way you communicate in a particular relationship, they become a pattern, a habit, a communication style. But even then, you aren't stuck. In the next moment, you can choose to communicate differently. You can be an Eagle.

But isn't that just my personality?

The way you communicate is not your personality. It's a behavior that may help you or others describe your personality. However, personality is an overall picture of who you are- a combination of preferences and behaviors. The way you communicate is just one of those behaviors. When we watch the way someone communicates, we use those observations to make conclusions about his or her personality.

I'm sure you've heard the idea that men typically have fewer words than women. My husband, Brian, is not a case in point. In fact, he typically has twice as many words as I do and he can strike up a conversation with virtually anyone. We are in a hotel room right now and he's talking to the maintenance guy who is vacuuming up a million little bugs on the ceiling that I let in by leaving the window screens open while we were at dinner. I had no idea what to say to the guy, other than, "I'm sorry I let all the bugs in." But my husband found out his name, how often he has to vacuum up bugs, and discussed the construction of windows and screens. Amazing. When people describe Brian, they usually say he's really friendly. And when they do, they are observing the way he communicates and then making conclusions about a part of his personality.

Conversely, one of the strongest factors in the way you choose to communicate is your personality. Personality tests include hints as to how you typically communicate with others. If you've ever taken one of these tests, go back and read your final assessment to see what hints you can find.

Let's look at Myers-Briggs,[1] for example. If you took the test and were pegged as an extrovert, or someone who gets energy from being with others, the assessment will tell you that you enjoy working through an issue by talking about it out loud with other people. If you're an introvert, however, the assessment explains that sometimes you would rather enjoy the ideas in your head than talk about them with others and get their feedback. Because of these preferences are built into our personalities, we then naturally make certain choices in the way we communicate.

While we can't choose our preferences, we *can* become aware of the way we communicate and choose to interact differently. Certainly, making choices that go against our natural instincts takes a great deal of intentionality. Yet, intentional introverts can still make the choice to engage others, ask questions, share what's in their heads, and ask for feedback. And, intentional extroverts can choose to be quiet and listen well as someone else shares.

Your God-given personality will also impact your approach to difficult conversations, especially if you tend to avoid or fight. Take Monica, for example. She admittedly has a quieter, more sensitive, compliant personality. When her friend Kristen became incessantly critical of her, Monica avoided expressing what she was really feeling. Afraid she would offend her friend and risk losing a friendship, Monica chose to hide her true heart like a Turtle.

And then there's Alex. With his more outgoing, bold personality, he unabashedly told his brother, Aaron, he was an idiot for voting for a particular political candidate. When Aaron became defensive and told him his political choices were none of Alex's business, Alex vehemently reiterated his name-calling, adding new, potent adjectives. He clearly felt most comfortable fighting aggressively like a Bulldog.

LET'S TALK 3

1. *Are you quiet, sensitive, and feelings-oriented? Or outgoing, bold and thinking-oriented? Or somewhere in between?*

2. *How do you think your particular personality affects your communication style?*

Besides your personality, there are other factors that play into the way you communicate, and especially the way you approach tough conversations. Such as...

Your Childhood

We each learned to communicate in a particular way with our parents and siblings and other family members. Over the years, we found it to be the most effective method to get our needs met and survive in our family of origin. Those patterns often continue as we become adults. Like David. He learned from an early age that expressing what he really wanted resulted in negative consequences, like a verbal kick in the gut or the silent treatment from his caregivers. Today, he tends to avoid tough conversations at all cost. For Christy, however, she learned from an early age that demanding what she wanted was the most effective way to get her needs met. Today, she tends to use tough conversations to assert herself and fight for her rights.

We all learned to choose the communication style that helped us feel safest as a child. I asked my very outspoken colleage, Peg, "I'll bet you were really outspoken in your family growing up, right?"

She said, "Oh no, I was a really quiet kid. Definitely a Turtle. The rest of my family was all Bulldogs."

"Wait. So you changed? So how did you become such a..."

"A Bulldog, you mean?" she laughed.

I was relieved. I had no interest in calling out a Bulldog. "You said it, not me."

She explained, "When I left home and went to college, I finally felt free to be who I really was. And that was outspoken."

We can all imagine what most of Peg's family members must have been like—loud and opinionated. And then there was Peg—afraid to say what she thought because she might get her head bitten off. Yet, deep down, she always had strong opinions. She had just learned to keep them under wraps.

If you think back on your childhood, there are probably certain instances you can remember in which you learned the safest way to communicate. And, you may have learned the hard way. Like me.

I'm 11. My sister and I sit in the back seat of the car, my mom and dad in the front as we drive through the tree-lined streets of a beautiful neighborhood. "Look at this neighborhood!" my dad says. "We should come back here and take a bike ride."

I think about that for a moment. Being a daddy's girl, I picture my dad and I riding down the streets together, laughing at silly squirrels, racing each other to the corner. And then, it suddenly strikes me that I would prefer to go on a bike ride there with my dad more than with my mom.

57

I wonder...I wonder what would happen if I actually said what I was thinking? It was a crazy thought. Incredibly risky. About as risky as walking into a field wearing a steel hat during a lightning storm. In a moment of calculated impulsivity, I decide to take the risk. My thoughts come tumbling out of my mouth. "I want to go on a bike ride here with you, dad, but not with mom."

My words hang in the air. I hold my breath. My mom keeps looking out the window. And then...the gavel strikes. Swiftly. "Thanks, Heidi."

Shame washes over me and then I instantly begin backpeddling, something like, "Wait, no. What I meant to say was that first I'll go on the bike ride with dad and then you and I can...wait, no, actually I don't even have to first do the bike ride just with dad, you can come too, Mom. We can all go together! That would be more fun anyway!"

I try desperately to grab the words back, rearrange them and distill out all the hurt before sending them back again. But the damage has been done. She is hurt. And I did the hurting.

When we arrive back at home, I step out of the car a committed Turtle, determined never again to say anything that will hurt my mother- even if it means hiding what I really think.

Today, I might be an adult, but everyone is my mother.

LET'S TALK 4
   1. As a child, how did your caregivers respond to your truth-telling?

2. How may the way your caregivers responded to you have influenced your approach today to difficult conversations?

3. Is there an instance you can remember from your childhood that shaped the way you tend to communicate today? If so, describe it here.

In *Why You Do What You Do*,[2] executive mentor Bob Biehl tells how he asked an animal trainer, "How can you tie a rope from a ten-ton elephant to a little bitty stake and that enormous animal won't try to get away?" The trainer explained that the little stake is the same stake they use with baby elephants to keep them in place. Once they learn they can't possibly get away, they never forget. Elephants really do have excellent memories, after all, and they never forget the power of the little stake, even when they weigh ten tons.

Like an elephant with an excellent memory, you, too, communicate the way you do because of your interactions in your family of origin.

But you also communicate the way you do because of another factor...

What You Want

We choose to communicate the way we do because it works- we've found it to be the best way to get what we want in the short run. In this, we must first differentiate between the short run and the long run. The short run is what we want NOW, and the long run is what we *ultimately* want. Yet, so often what we want in the short run trumps what we want in the long run. Let me illustrate.

If one of my boys asks for a cookie and I say, "Nope, sorry, buddy, it's almost dinnertime," he may try stomping his foot and yelling, "Give me a cookie, NOW!" But he'll quickly learn that's only going to get him some much-needed alone time in his room. I know what he really wants in the long run is connection with me, yet he sabotages that chance for connection because of his short-run desire for a cookie.

Like babies, we all start out crying, even screaming, demanding what we want the moment we want it. Perhaps we are all born Bulldogs. Some of us have continued to use the "Bulldog" method and have found that demanding what we want, loudly and forcefully, works quite well. People quickly give us the cookie. Others of us have had a different experience- demanding what we want only gets us rejection and disconnection. So the pendulum swings to the other side. We don't even ask for the cookie; we just look at them longingly and hope they'll give us one.

There are also those of us who have found that neither demanding like a Bulldog nor hiding like a Turtle get us what we want. And so we try to be clever- like a Fox. Like saying, "I really like cookies," while licking our lips, in hopes our indirect attempt will garner us a cookie from a sympathetic soul. Or we might try sneaking a cookie and eating it behind the couch.

One evening, a little mouth told me, "I didn't eat a cookie," but the evidence was quite visible in the form of crumbs and chocolate on his little face. "You're telling me the truth that you didn't eat a cookie?" I asked.

"No!" he declared.

"Then what's that on your face? It looks like a cookie to me."

"It's not *a* cookie, Mommy. It's three cookies."

If we really, really want the cookie, we're willing to risk what we want in the long run for what we want in the short run.

LET'S TALK 5

1. *What are some daily things you want in the short run? (i.e. money, a clean house, an attentive friend or spouse, etc.)*

2. *How do you use fear-based communication (the Turtle, Fox, or Bulldog) to help you get what you want in the short run?*

CREATIVE EXERCISE- "The Chair" (during small group)

During this exercise, you'll try as many different communication strategies as possible to get a person out of a chair and sit in it yourself. Or, you may be the person sitting in the chair who refuses to get up. Discuss what works, what doesn't, and the difference between what you want in the short run and the long run.

We all have strategies we use to get what we want in the short run. If one doesn't work, we try another. But what do we want in the long run? For the actual creatures- turtles, bulldogs, or foxes, in both the short and the long run they want to stay alive. And with that goal in mind, they find ways to capture food to eat and defend themselves from being eaten. They know it's dangerous to be found vulnerable, so they utilize various defense mechanisms. A turtle hides safely under a hard shell so that a predator will have a much more difficult time getting to the edible part. A bulldog bares sharp fangs so predators will be afraid and run away. And a fox sneaks around under the cover of night so as not to be seen stalking the chickens.

Just like us. Our hiding and baring and sneaking in the way we communicate are defense mechanisms we've learned to use to stay alive, to protect ourselves from people who we believe could potentially hurt us. So, in the short and the long run, we don't want to be hurt and we want to stay alive. But let's look a little deeper.

Thompson writes that "through the process of emotion," we long "to be connected to others."[3] As babies, it was when we were connected to our caregivers that our needs were met. So we cried, hoping an adult would notice and connect with us. As the adult met our physical and emotional needs, we experienced connection, which led to a better quality of life.

Not surprisingly, scientific research confirms our longing for connection, such as the article in the New York Times in the 1980's that revealed how premature babies who were touched were healthier than those who were isolated without touch.[4] Today, parents of premature babies are encouraged to massage those tiny hands and feet. We need connection in order to thrive. We need connection and we don't want to lose it.

"If we are not so sure of our connection, it starts a negative spiral of insecurity that chills the relationship," writes Dr. Sue Johnson in her book, *Hold Me Tight*.[5] It might be a certain tone of voice, a particular word or phrase, a leaning away, a look. By reading the nonverbal and verbal signals of the other person, we might come to the conclusion that our connection is in jeopardy. And if we are disconnected, we will experience the shame of loneliness, abandonment, and rejection.

And then we feel afraid.

Our fear fuels primitive responses, responses that are ignited by the amygdala, a crazy-strong, almond-shaped cluster of nuclei deep in the brain. One of my friends, Jill Baird, who is a researcher and a therapist, explains how scientists have linked the amygdala to how we respond to fear.[6] Our primitive fight or flight responses originate in that little cluster of nuclei. You can tell yourself all day long to go into a tough conversation with a calm heart and a clear head but if your amygdala senses a threat, it fires off messages to your brain that tell it to jumpstart your fear-based communication style to protect your connection in that relationship.[7]

And so, compelled by our fear, we hide, or sneak, or fight in the way we communicate. However, can you see the problem? Do any of these methods result in true connection? If the Turtle hides and isn't known, deep connection isn't possible. If the Fox sneaks, using indirect methods that shame the other person, deep connection isn't possible. And, if the Bulldog fights and scares away the other person, deep connection isn't possible either. Our default communication choices that are rooted in fear ultimately sabotage our most important relationships.

LET'S TALK 6

1. *What are some things you want in the long run?*

2. *Can you think of a time when the way you communicated sabotaged what you really wanted in the long run? Describe it.*

WORDS FROM THE WORD – JOHN 10:27-30, EPH. 4:11-16

The beauty of the gospel is that, regardless of our tenuous connections with people here on earth, we have an unbreakable connection with God through our Good Shepherd, Jesus Christ.

Read John 10:27-30

1. *How can knowing that no one can snatch you out of Jesus'*
   hand give you the courage to make new choices in the way
   you communicate?

Read Eph. 4:11-16.

2. *Given your communication tendencies, is it more difficult*
   for you to speak the truth or to speak love? Why?

3. *Why do you think "speaking the truth in love" and "grow"*
   are in the same verse?

4. *What other observations can you make about the biblical*
   context of the phrase "speaking the truth in love?"

Like John, Becky, and Bob, we all have difficult people and situations in our lives that require us to have tough conversations. And, as risky as they feel, they are opportunities for us to grow in our faith and in our ability to be an Eagle, to speak the truth in love and stay focused on what we want in the long run. With God's help, we can make Eagle choices to engage honestly and respond to each other in such a way that honors God, fosters trust, and keeps the connections alive in our relationships. In the following chapter, we'll take a closer look into the motivations of my little creature of choice- The Turtle.

As we end this session, let's pray.

TALK TO GOD

Pray for...

> *humility to recognize when your communication choices are rooted in fear*

> *wisdom to know what you really want in the long run- and what God wants*
> *for you*

> *ears to hear how your default communication style may be sabotaging your most important relationships*

> *and the faith to believe you are secure in the arms of Jesus.*

SESSION FOUR
The Turtle

Corrie sat down in her aisle seat, slid her carry-on under the seat in front of her, and buckled her seatbelt. She was looking forward to using this flight to disappear into a good book. The 40-something woman next to her was already engrossed in SkyMall.

"Brrr!" she thought, and looked up. Arctic air was blasting out of the vent directly above her seat. Let that stay on for too long and she'd soon have icicles hanging off her nose hairs. She reached up and twisted the vent shut. "Whew, that's better," she thought. She looked down and opened her book.

Suddenly, she was re-blasted by the freezing air! She looked back up. "That's weird," she thought. "I'm sure I closed it." She glanced at the woman next to her. Yep, still flipping through SkyMall. Corrie reached up, twisted the vent shut again and looked back down at her book.

Then, out of the corner of her eye, she saw it. The arm of the woman next to her- lightning fast- reached up and twisted Corrie's vent back open! Corrie glanced up, shocked, and then stared at the woman, wide-eyed, trying to nonverbally hand her an F for airplane etiquette. The woman realized she had been caught.

"Oh, it's just way too hot in here to keep that vent closed!" the woman blustered, fanning herself with her magazine.

Corrie knew she should say something. She really wanted to say something. She was freezing and uncomfortable. She debated in her mind, "It's *my* air vent. I have the right to keep it shut. But is it really worth it to fight with this woman? No. It isn't. And it's just for a few hours. I'll just...I'll just fold my arms...like this."

And so, my dear friend Corrie sat with her arms folded and froze...for the entire flight.

"So you never said anything?" I asked over lunch, as Corrie finished her story.

"I know I should have!" Corrie's voice rose. "That was so wrong of her! And I was absolutely freezing. But I just couldn't bring myself to say anything." She took a sip of her iced tea. "Funny thing is, I was standing up for myself in my mind. Do you know, I even have dreams of standing up for myself?"

We talked about communication patterns. She took the assessment in Session Three. And neither of us were surprised to find that her default style was the Turtle. She admitted that her choices were rooted in fear.

"Do you have to capitalize Turtle?" she winced, playfully. "I would like it better if it were lowercase." Then her face turned serious. "I've been this way my whole life. But I really want to get stronger."

LET'S TALK 1
What would you have done on that airline flight? Would you have stayed quiet like Corrie? Why or why not?

If you prefer to communicate like a Turtle, you understand Corrie's predicament. Be quiet and freeze, or speak and risk a fight. For some of us, freezing seems much less scary than fighting. If you are a Fox or a Bulldog, you don't understand Corrie at all. You would fight. And you would win. Period.

Compliant and submissive, Turtles hide what they really think at the first sign of a threat. But these easily startled creatures come in varying shades of passivity. While one person might communicate consistently in passive ways across all their relationships, another might choose to communicate passively only with one particular person once in a while. So let's look at this pattern as a continuum with many points along the line.

To find out where you have fallen on the Turtle continuum in the past, take the following quiz, made up of 10 questions. And before you say, "I'm not taking this quiz because I know this isn't me," I dare you to try it, just for fun. Even assertive communicators might choose to hide their heads in their shells once in a while.

THE TURTLE QUIZ

On the following quiz, score yourself from 1-5 for each statement, with 1 being Almost Never, and 5 being Almost Always. Then, total your points at the end of the quiz.

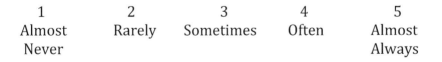

1	2	3	4	5
Almost Never	Rarely	Sometimes	Often	Almost Always

_____I have tried not to disagree with others, especially when they have strong opinions

_____It has been hard for me to stand up for myself

_____I have avoided verbal confrontation

_____It has made me nervous to assert my opinion

_____People have taken advantage of me because I didn't say what I was really thinking and feeling

_____It has been hard for me to say "No" to someone with a strong personality

_____I have felt guilty when I have asked for what I need, especially if I have known it's going to inconvenience someone else

_____If I have thought it might start a fight, I have chosen not to say anything

_____I have tried to say what other people want to hear

_____I have chosen to hide what I really thought or felt, rather than risk hurting someone else's feelings

Total: _____

What Your Score Means
If you scored 10-20, you are rarely a Turtle; it's not very often that you choose to use a passive communication style to attempt to get what you want. In your experience, you have found one of the other communication choices to be the most effective.

If you scored 20-35, you sometimes are a Turtle; occasionally you use a passive communication style to attempt to get what you want. With certain people and situations you are able to communicate assertively, but with other situations you feel safest not revealing what you really think.

If you scored 35-50, you are usually a Turtle; this passive communication style is your pattern of choice when you are afraid. You have found it to be the safest and most effective way to get what you want in the short run, which is usually NO CONFLICT.

LET'S TALK 2
   1. *What was your score?*

   2. *Are you rarely, sometimes, or usually a Turtle?*

   3. *Does this ring true for you?*

How Does a Turtle Communicate?
   This communication style is marked by four characteristics: Indirect, Complying, Stuffing, and Snapping.

Indirect
   My colleague, Peg, is a corporate trainer on social styles. As we were talking one day about the differences between the ways we each communicate, she said that she liked to call the passive style, "Ask," as opposed to "Tell."
   Yeah, tell me about it.
   On Friday nights we have often hosted neighborhood meals in our home. One Friday night, I realized another couple was about to come in the door and we needed to make room at the table for them. So, I asked Doug, who sat across

the table from me, "Hey, would you mind scooting over a seat?"

One eyebrow went up as he retorted, "What if I do mind?"

I knew he was giving me a hard time. I smiled, "Okay, fine. I need you to move over a seat."

He scooted over. "Then just tell me to move over."

Doug is clearly not a Turtle. If he were, he would understand how being direct and *telling* him to do something goes completely against my nature. I much prefer to be indirect and *ask* him to scoot over.

But even asking sometimes feels too aggressive. So I might string a bunch of qualifiers together when asking someone to do something, such as "Do you think you could possibly consider maybe taking your shoe off my big toe?"

When I explained my hesitancy to ask direct questions in a recent small group, one woman named Candy said she's very suspicious of Turtles. "When you ask me to do something in a roundabout way it makes me not trust you. Stop doing that! Just ask me!" The Turtles in the room were incredulous. And here we all thought we were being extra polite!

LET'S TALK 3
Do you find that you prefer to communicate directly or indirectly?

Why do you think that is?

For some of us, asking can sometimes feel risky. Risky because someone could say no. Sometimes we're so afraid of hearing a "no" that we don't ask at all. We just keep our heads hidden safely in our shells. But if we get up the courage to peek our heads out and ask and someone replies, "No," well, then that leads to the next element that characterizes the way the Turtle communicates.

Complying

When you choose the passive communication style, you use words that comply with the demands of others, agreeing to what they want you to do. Such as, "Okay, sure! I'll sit there." (That is, behind the pillar where you can't see).

Other times you don't use words at all but still communicate compliance by doing what the other person wants you to do, even when it's not the choice you really want to make. It's a bit like the corporate world in which "compliance" means obeying industry-specific regulations in order to keep a company afloat. But in this case, you are obeying relationship-specific regulations. Regulations which you think are necessary to keep the connection in your relationship alive.

And, because you think compliance is necessary for connection, you are willing to do things you don't want to do. Like go to a concert to hear a band you don't like. Or eat key lime pie when you hate key lime pie. Or stop to visit someone when you would rather go home.

I used to think that compliance was a good thing. It meant I was the good girl, the nice girl, the Christian girl, the girl who was agreeable all the time. And then I met my husband.

One night, we were on the way home from an evening out and my pastor- husband Brian asked if we could stop and say hello to another family in town. We were newly married and being the agreeable wife that I am, I said, "Sure!"

But as we turned the corner into their neighborhood, I yawned. He looked at me. "You sure you're up for this?"

I smiled back at him. "Yeah, of course."

But he was getting to know me. "Do you really want to go see them, or are you just saying that because you know it's what I want to hear?"

I had been caught. He pulled over. "Heidi. Tell me what you really want to do."

I sucked in my breath. It felt like the scariest moment, ever. It wasn't about anything monumental, like telling him I didn't want to have children or something, it was about telling him what I really thought about an ordinary visit to a nice family for 30 minutes. And yet, it felt like I was standing right on the edge of the Empire State Building about to jump.

"You really want to know what I want?" I asked, looking down at my shoes.

He nodded, "I really want to know what you want."

I turned and looked at him. His eyes told me he wanted to know me. Not the compliant me, but the real me.

"Umm, well, I guess I don't really want to stop and visit them. I guess I would rather just go home." I held my breath. Surely he would shame me for being so selfish.

But he didn't. He smiled. "Okay, then we'll go home." And we did.

Shortly after that, a counselor gave me the book, *Boundaries*,[1] by Dr. Henry Cloud and Dr. John Townsend. It totally rocked my world. In that book, I learned that compliance was tied to a lack of boundaries. They write, "compliant people have fuzzy and indistinct boundaries; they 'melt' into the demands and needs of other people."

Wait, what? I thought I was just being nice. What did boundaries have to do with it?

One of my first counselors, Jennifer VanOrman, explained that your life is like a yard with a fence around it and a gate in the fence. You use the gate to protect yourself by keeping the bad out and letting the good in. Inside your fence are all of your feelings and wants and needs. And here's the kicker: you are only responsible for what is inside your fence.

When you're being compliant, you often don't protect or take responsibility for what is inside your fence. Take me, for instance, in the car with my husband on our way to visit another family. I'm an introvert, I was peopled-out, and I wanted to go home. But initially I didn't communicate in a way to protect myself and what I needed. In fact, I felt responsible for what was inside my husband's fence- his experience of happiness. And, to make sure he was happy, I assessed the feelings that were inside my fence, thought they didn't fit with the relationship-specific regulations (making my husband happy), and came up with new feelings that were safe to express ("Sure!"), even though they weren't the truth.

Or, consider Corrie's situation. She didn't "shut the gate" and protect herself from freezing but instead took responsibility for the other woman's comfort, even though it was within her rights to insist on closing her own vent. By allowing her vent (and her gate) to remain open, she also opened herself up to pain- the pain of freezing.

How often do Turtles keep the gate open when they should close it? Often. That's probably because of how hard it is for us to say the little two-letter word, "No." In her book *Codependent No More*, author Melody Beattie writes that compliant people even go as far as to "eliminate the word 'no' from their vocabulary."[2] But she didn't just call us Turtles compliant- she called us "codependent." Thank you very much, Melody. Compliant sounds kind of nice; codependent sounds...rather, unhealthy. She defines codependents as people who let other people's behavior affect them. Codependents aren't just Turtles- they can be the other communication styles, too. But, if you typically communicate like a Turtle, you probably let the behavior of others affect the way you communicate by staying silent or by telling others what they want to hear.

LET'S TALK 4
Do you typically feel responsible for the emotions inside other people's fences? Why or why not?

The problem is, as much as we believe it's the safest choice to tell others what they want to hear, our true feelings don't go away. We have to put them somewhere. So, we stuff them, which brings us to the next characteristic that describes the way the Turtle communicates.

Stuffing
Turtles wear a sign over their faces split in half- half of the sign is a happy face and the other half a question mark. For Turtles, a smile doesn't necessarily mean we're happy. It might mean we are stuffing our real feelings and cleverly covering them over with a smile.

Some of us stuff them because we convince ourselves our feelings aren't good or right. I remember one of my first marriage counseling sessions. I said, "Sometimes I get really mad. But I know I shouldn't feel that way." Jeff Helton, our counselor, looked across his desk at my husband and me. Actually, he just looked at me. He said, "Heidi, you're emotions are what they are. You can't censor them and tell yourself they're bad and you can't tell yourself not to feel them. They are what they are. You do feel them and they have to go somewhere."

Others of us stuff them because we convince ourselves our thoughts and feelings aren't important enough to mention. Corrie told me, "If someone hurts me, I can talk myself out of saying anything. I just tell myself, 'It's not that big of a deal.'"

Sometimes we stuff them because it's just not worth the risk of letting the other person know. Like Allan. I met Alan in a graduate course I was teaching. An intelligent, well-spoken professional, Allan had worked in the same company for over 15 years. He wrote in one of his papers that his boss was a man with "little patience," who "used his arms-length position to bring his will to bear." Because Allan was "conflict-averse," as he described himself, he rarely told his boss what he was really thinking. He had seen what happened to other people who disagreed or confronted his boss in some way- they lost their jobs. And he didn't want to risk being kicked to the curb, too.

Or Jeannie. Jeannie is smart, fun, beautiful, and successful. But she has learned to avoid disagreeing with her husband on anything. As a lawyer with a very strong personality, he is extremely persuasive and is able to take apart her arguments or justify his actions with great skill. As we talked the other day, she told me that she has been trying to be an agreeable wife but has actually just been stuffing her true feelings for over 10 years. Now, she says she's done. Something has to change or she's leaving.

Stuffing is only a temporary fix. Eventually, the unspoken emotions become a boiling time bomb of anger and distrust and hurt and fear. One last jab at the smile on the sign and suddenly the last remaining second on the ticking clock reaches 00:00. It's then that we find out what was really under the question mark all along.

The Turtle has snapped.

Snapping

A while ago, I read Donald Miller's book, *Scary Close*. He suggests, "The deeper you fuse your soul to somebody, the more damage you do when you become a bomb."[4]

A bomb. A destructive bomb. And perhaps the longer we stuff, the bigger the explosion. Or the harder the snap. Our explosions especially surprise those who know us as the nice, agreeable people we usually are. Kind of like the turtle who surprised me a few years ago.

I was driving along, with two of my little boys in car seats in the back, when I suddenly saw a creature in the middle of the road ahead of me. It was a turtle.

"Oh no! That sweet little turtle is going to get hit!" I told my little ones. And then, being the rescuer-of-the-helpless that I am and wanting to show my kids that we are kind to animals, I pulled over. "Wait here," I told them.

I stepped out and walked towards the little guy. Only, as I began to realize, he wasn't a little guy at all. He was a big guy. In fact, he was the biggest turtle I had ever seen. He was so big I wasn't sure I would even be able to lift him. I looked back and saw a car approaching. I needed to act fast. I reached down to pick him up and suddenly the turtle whirled his head around towards me, hissing.

"Hey, mister! I'm trying to rescue you!" I muttered. The approaching car had stopped and the driver was clearly watching. Now, along with my own boys who were watching out my car windows, I had an audience.

I waved at the driver and pointed down at the creature, yelling, "Turtle! I'm rescuing him!" He waved back. Then I reached back down and assertively grasped the two sides of his enormous shell.

Bad idea. He whirled his head around again and this time he snapped at me! Wide open mouth, powerful jaws, faster-than-lightning. "What in the world?" I pulled my hands back just as the driver of the other car yelled out his window, "Be careful! That's a snapping turtle!"

Yeah, thanks, guy. I figured that out. I backed away from the turtle carefully and got in my car, my heart racing. Thankfully, I still had all my fingers. And then I drove off, explaining to my very confused children that sometimes turtles snap.

Think back to the times you stuffed your feelings for a while and then suddenly snapped ferociously at the people in your life and hurt them with your words. I'll bet they were shocked, dumbfounded at how such a nice, controlled, agreeable person like you could lose it in such a dramatic way. And you probably ended up feeling ashamed for snapping.

Like Julie. Suffering from her teenage angst, she verbally exploded all over her family and then ran to her room and slammed the door. Her mother promptly took some flowers out of a vase in their dining room and stood at her closed bedroom door. When Julie opened the door, there her family was, holding the flowers and clapping for her excellent performance. Julie felt stupid for having snapped. And then berated herself and went back to hiding in her shell.

The responses of others can tend to entrench our communication patterns a little more deeply. When someone invalidates our emotions, snaps back, or even gets violent, we decide our Turtle ways are the safest and go back to hiding and stuffing and eventually...snapping again.

LET'S TALK 6

Describe a time you snapped. What might have led to you snapping?

What's the Turtle so afraid of?

We could say we hide what we really think not because we are afraid of something but because we want harmony. Truly, our desire for harmony is a positive way to state what we want. But what is the other side of harmony? Conflict. Turtles are "conflict-averse," as my student Allan described himself. Conflict feels scary.

Scary. That's fear. But let's not stop there. Let's peel off a few more layers.

So, what's so scary about conflict? If you're a Turtle, think about how conflict feels for you. You state what you think and the other person disagrees, you state what you feel and the other person tells you that you shouldn't feel that way. In fact, you feeling that way might even make the other person feel bad about him or herself. And then you feel guilty for making the other person feel bad.

When people disagree with us or feel badly about themselves because of something we said, they might raise their voices, look away, say harsh words, give us the silent treatment, even speak poorly about us to other people. Put all of that together and we could say it might look at lot like they are...rejecting us.

Ah...so we're afraid of rejection. Disconnection. Shame.

Wait. What does shame have to do with it? Shame is that feeling that something is wrong with me. That I'm defective in some way. And that my intrinsic defects are the reason why I'm being rejected. In order to guarantee we don't have to experience the shame of disconnection we don't share anything that might lead to us being rejected. If we can hide what we really think we can then control the responses of the other person and thereby protect ourselves from experiencing shame.

In the past, I've looked at people who seem to tend towards the other fear-based communication styles- like the Bulldog- and felt a bit self-righteous. I rarely bite anyone's head off. I'm the friendly Turtle who never makes any waves.

Oh, but how deceptive is my own pride. A few years ago, I went through the soul-wracking study, *Gospel Transformation*,[5] and learned that we are all control freaks in our own way. Our choice to communicate like Turtles is not because we're such nice people; it's because we want to control what others think of us, what they say to us, and how they act toward us. Instead of controlling you with verbal force, like a Bulldog, I control you by not saying anything. I keep my head safely in my shell, poking it out occasionally to smile at you so you'll like me. So you won't criticize me. So you won't yell at me. So you won't reject me.

If you're a Turtle, when you sense that your connection is in jeopardy, that you could be headed toward experiencing that chilly insecurity you hate so much, your amygdala sends out a fear signal and ignites your primitive response of hiding. You then retreat further into your shell and determine that hiding with some shred of connection is better than honesty that results in the shame of disconnection.

Yet, all of this begs the question- if we run from hard conversations by hiding what we really think and feel and who we really are, can we truly have a heart connection with the other person?

I thought it could work. I thought I could hide in my shell in the way I communicated with others and still experience real connection. But I finally came to the sad realization that all my hiding hadn't gained me the intimacy I so desired. That's the desperately tragic truth about choosing to communicate like a Turtle- in the end, the connection we imagine we have is just a sham. When we are hiding, we aren't truly known. And when we never allow anyone to really know us, we never get what we really wanted in the first place: true connection.

How can faith help the Turtle become an Eagle?

The Turtle hides because he or she deeply fears rejection and disconnection. But what if we have already been ultimately accepted? What if the ultimate connection is already in place and can never again be severed? The truth is, no matter how much rejection we experience here on this earth, the rejection of others can never touch the power of God's ultimate acceptance of us. God tells us in Isaiah 43:1,

"Fear not, for I have redeemed you; I have called you by name; you are Mine." He wants you. He loves you. He accepts you. And that's forever.

Forever.

In John 10:28, Jesus promises that if you have trusted in Him for your salvation, He will give you eternal life so that you will never perish and no one can snatch you out of His hand. How do we know this is true? We believe it by faith.

Look back at Isaiah 43:1. In my paraphrase, the verse begins with, "Don't be afraid." Why? God says, "Because I've got you. You're mine." As we believe by faith in our unbreakable connection with God, our fear of speaking up can't help but dissolve into His love, for "...perfect love casts out fear..." (I John 4:18).

If only Moses had known this.

WORDS FROM THE WORD
Read Exodus 3-4:17

1. *After reading this passage, what are some adjectives you would use to describe Moses' communication style at this point in his life?*

We know Moses as a great man of faith who fearlessly led the Israelites through the Red Sea and across the wilderness to the Promised Land. I picture him bravely holding up his staff to part the Red Sea, furiously smashing the Ten Commandments. But there was a time when he was held captive by fear.

Imagine Moses, his bare feet in the dust, wind blowing hot against his face from the burning bush, terrified at God's voice telling him to go back to the palace where he lived as a child and have an extremely tough conversation with Pharoah.

Sometimes we might wonder if it's the right thing to approach a friend or coworker or a boss or a loved one with words that might cause a conflict, but in Moses's case, there was no doubt this was what God wanted him to do. God spoke audibly and told him to go to Pharoah and "...bring My people, the sons of Israel, out of Egypt" (Ex. 3:10).

Yet, even though Moses heard God's voice and even made his staff become a snake, He was still afraid. He asked God, "Who am I, that I should go to Pharoah...?" and later, in my paraphrase, he pleaded with God, "Please, Lord, I have never been good at speaking, not recently, not a long time ago, and not even now since you started talking to me from the bush." In other words- "Don't make me do this! I'm a Turtle! I would be much happier hiding my head safely in my shell than having to say something that would cause a fight with Pharoah!"

But "The Lord said to him, "Who has made man's mouth? Or who makes him mute or deaf, or seeing or blind? Is it not I, the LORD? Now then go, and I, even I, will be with your mouth, and teach you what you are to say" (Ex. 4:11-12).

Even with these promises from God, Moses was still afraid and pleaded with God, I imagine in a whiny voice, "Can't You just send someone else?" And so God allowed Aaron, Moses' brother, to be His mouthpiece.

2. *What do you think Moses was so afraid of? Look for clues in Scripture.*

Read Exodus 32:21-26

Later in His life, we see Moses speak to the Israelites in a whole new way when he finds them worshipping a golden calf they had made. He gives them a choice, shouting, "Whoever is for the LORD, *come* to me!" (Ex. 32:26)

3. *What are some adjectives that describe Moses's new style of communication?*

4. *What were some events Moses would have experienced between Exodus 3 and 32 that undoubtedly gave him new confidence in the way he communicated?*

Clearly, Moses had become a Courageous Eagle, learning to trust that God was with Him, to say what God asked Him to say, and not worry about his lack of eloquence

85

or rejection. In fact, I have a feeling by Exodus 32:26, he wasn't even thinking about being eloquent; he was only thinking about following God. When you find yourself anticipating a hard conversation, conquer your fear of rejection and disconnection with faith, reminding yourself that God has accepted you unconditionally and eternally and that your connection with Him is unbreakable.

Remind yourself of these truths like my graduate student, Allan, who wrote in his paper, "I am now more willing to take chances as my decisions are from my confidence in God's place in my life." Or like Corrie, who is now taking newfound steps of faith to set boundaries and communicate confidently to protect her own heart from harm- and her body from freezing air vents.

As for the woman who kept opening Corrie's air vent, she needs to read ahead to the next two sessions in this book: The Fox and the Bulldog.

LET'S TALK 7
In what relationship is God asking you speak out, trusting that He fully accepts you?

CREATIVE EXERCISES- "Turtle Pledge" and "Do-Over" (during small group time)

You will be invited to stand, put your hand over your heart, and recite each phrase of the following "Turtle Pledge:"

THE TURTLE PLEDGE

"I am done with hiding. I am ready to walk out of my shell and stand up for myself, for what I think, feel, and need. My voice is valuable, and I promise to use it in life-giving ways for myself and others. I will not be afraid of rejection, because I am accepted fully by God through Jesus Christ. He is my Good Shepherd and I will trust Him."

Along with this, your small group leader will give group members an opportunity to go back and "redo" any recent conversations in which they hid, now practicing what it could have been like to speak the truth in love.

TALK TO GOD

After the Creative Exercise, spend some time in prayer as a group. Pray for any specific relationships or situations that were expressed in LET'S TALK 7 and then pray that you would...

show empathy for any Turtles in your life

have the faith to believe you are fully accepted by God

confess your desire to control others with your silence

walk humbly and confidently into any difficult conversations this week

and believe God for what He can do in you and through you!

SESSION FIVE
The Fox

Shari opens the front of the dishwasher, "click," and lets the door fall, "slam." She stacks the plates on one arm, "clang, clang, clang," and then opens the cupboard, stacking the plates on the shelf, "clank, clank, clank, clank." Then, she lets the cupboard door "slam." On purpose.

She opens the drawer, "scrrrape," takes handfuls of silverware out of the dishwasher and jams the forks, knives, and spoons in their allotted spots, "ching, ching, ching, ching." Every noise she makes is a mad word, and even though she doesn't speak them, Shari hopes she is making each word perfectly clear to the man in the living room.

The man in the living room is her husband, Stan. He's focused on the news on the screen with his feet propped up on the coffee table. Since he doesn't seem to hear what she isn't saying, she gets louder. "SLAM!" goes the drawer. Stan jumps.

"Honey? Everything okay in there?"

Since he doesn't turn around, he can't see the steam coming out of her ears. She tightens her jaw and mutters back through clenched teeth, "Everything's fine."

"Hey, do we have any more of that mint and chip ice cream?" he asks.

"I don't know, Stan. Maybe you could look." Shari scrubs pasta remains off the bottom of a pot, rinses it, and flips it upside down into the dish drainer with a "thwunk."

"Just asking," he says.

She wipes off the counters, slaps the washcloth on the side of the sink, and marches through the living room. "I'm going to bed."

He looks up at her. "You sure you're okay? You seem edgy."

She keeps marching, headed for the stairs. "Yeah, well, I wonder why."

He looks confused. "Yeah, me, too. Wanna fill me in?"

She tosses back, "I shouldn't have to."

He rolls his eyes. "Okaaay."

She marches up the stairs, but stops midway, listening. No footsteps. No indicator that he is pursuing her, trying to figure out what he did wrong, trying to make things right.

She gets ready for bed and climbs between crisp sheets- alone.

"Did you ever tell him what you were mad about?" I ask Shari as we sit by our neighborhood pool, talking.

"Yeah, I gave him the silent treatment the next day and then he finally made me tell him."

I can guess, but I ask anyway. "What was it?"

"I was mad that I was doing the dishes and he was watching TV. I wanted him to come clean the kitchen with me."

That's what I figured. "So it didn't work?"

She laughs, "Actually the next night I slammed the drawers a little louder, and, guess what? He came out and helped me."

LET'S TALK 1
If you were Shari, wanting to get Stan's attention to come help you clean the kitchen, how would you have communicated what you wanted?

If you typically communicate like a Fox, you understand Shari's predicament. Taking the passive approach and hiding what you feel completely seems impossible. However, taking the aggressive approach by demanding that the other person help you feels way too risky. So you choose the middle ground: passive-aggressive. With carefully chosen words and actions, the Fox doesn't communicate outright, but sneaks in through the back door with a clever method that still does the job. Foxes don't mean to be sneaky; it's just that passive-aggression feels like the safest way to attempt to get what they want.

As you're reading this, I have a feeling you're thinking of the people in your personal life or workplace you would label a Fox. But hang on- let's look a little closer at the way *you* communicate. Even if you typically consider yourself a Turtle or a Bulldog, there still might be times you choose to be passive-aggressive. Like the other communication styles, let's look at the Fox as a continuum with many points along the line.

To find out where you might fall on the Fox continuum, take the following quiz, made up of 10 questions. And before you say, "I'm not taking this quiz because I've never been and will never be a Fox," I dare you to try it, just for fun. Truth be told, even typically passive or aggressive communicators might choose passive-aggression once in a while given the right situation.

THE FOX QUIZ

To find out how much passive-aggression affects the way you communicate, take the quiz below. Because none of us really want to admit being a Fox, this is the toughest quiz to take honestly. However, to get the most out of this chapter, I encourage you to really consider each statement thoughtfully and then answer as honestly as possible. I believe we all have a little Fox in us.

Answer each question with a number between 1 and 5, with 1 being Almost Never and 5 being Almost Always.

1	2	3	4	5
Almost Never	Rarely	Sometimes	Often	Almost Always

_____When I have needed something, I have preferred not to state it outright, but to give clues that I hoped the other person would understand

_____I have quietly kept my distance for a while to let someone know I was hurt or angry

_____Instead of making statements that would offend, I have asked pointed questions that communicate the same idea

_____I have used shame effectively to persuade another person to do what I wanted him or her to do

_____When someone enacts a change I don't agree with, I prefer not to express my disapproval directly but instead find other ways to resist the change

_____I have made things sound a little better or worse than they really were to get a certain reaction from another person

_____I have expressed neutral statements in just the right way so the other person knows what I really mean

_____If accused, I have turned things around to help the other person see his or her role in the matter

_____I have used my words, tone of voice, and facial expressions to help others sense their responsibility for how I was feeling

_____When I've been frustrated or disappointed, I have told someone else instead of expressing what I feel directly to the person responsible

Total: _____

What Your Score Means

If you scored 10-20, you are rarely a Fox; you infrequently choose to use a passive-aggressive communication style to attempt to get what you want. In your experience, you have found one of the other communication styles to be the most effective.

If you scored 20-35, you sometimes are a Fox; occasionally you use a passive-aggressive communication style to attempt to get what you want. You probably lean towards one of the other styles a good deal of the time, but then, there are certain people and situations that tend to bring out the Fox in you.

If you scored 35-50, you are usually a Fox; this passive-aggressive communication style is your style of choice when you're afraid. I applaud you for being willing to score yourself honestly. With your score in this range, it's clear that you have learned that being passive-aggressive is the safest and most effective way to get what you want.

It's interesting to take this quiz for yourself. It might be even more interesting to ask someone close to you to take this quiz with you in mind. Okay, that wouldn't just be interesting; it would be scary. The truth is, we can self-report anything we want. So, our self-reported Fox score may or may not be accurate. If you want a more accurate score, take a big risk and ask a family member or close friend to rate your degree of Foxy communication. You might be surprised at how much or how little the other person perceives your passive-aggressive communication choices are affecting your relationships.

LET'S TALK 2

1. *What was your score on The Fox Quiz?*

2. *Are you rarely a Fox, sometimes a Fox, or usually a Fox?*

3. *Does this ring true for you?*

How does a Fox communicate?

We all know Foxes to be those sneaky creatures that slink in under the cover of night and kill all the chickens. But before you judge them as malicious, it's important to understand that they have merely found this strategic style to be the safest way to communicate what they think and feel and get what they want. Often they have tried the passive style and tried the aggressive style, only to find those styles weren't received well or they kept finding themselves on the losing end of an interaction. So, they have developed a pattern that feels safe and more socially acceptable to them for this particular relationship.

Foxes are difficult to spot because they blend in with the background and they move so stealthily that you often don't know one has been present until you see or experience the aftermath. And, if you are the Fox, that is especially true. You often don't know you have communicated like a Fox until someone points out your style or responds in a way that makes you aware of your choice. That's because of the first characteristic of the Fox is Indirect.

Indirect

Like the Turtle, the Fox also communicates in an indirect way. However, while the Turtle might shrink from communicating at all, the Fox communicates what he or she is thinking and feeling indirectly through tone of voice, facial expressions, body language, and action. Like Shari at the beginning of this chapter, who made a whole lot of noise in the kitchen to attempt to get her husband to help her, the Fox communicates, but not in direct words.

With this indirect form of expression, the Fox can avoid being accused of aggression or hostility because those more negative traits are veiled behind seemingly innocuous statements and easily deniable actions. If accused, the Fox can easily slide out from under a pointed finger. Shari's answer to Stan's question about the mint and chip ice cream is a case in point. She responded, "I don't know, Stan. Maybe you could look." Said with enough punch, Stan would get her meaning without her having to say outright, "I'm not your servant. Look yourself, you lazy bum." And, if he dared to accuse her of meanness, she could easily say, "Honey, all I said was that I didn't know and I suggest you look."

If we find ourselves identifying with the Fox, we know it can be easy to convince even ourselves that our communication is merely truthful and therefore harmless. After all, the words themselves are neutral, right? However, we know deep down that they are laced with meaning that expresses our seemingly less attractive, hidden emotions, and are meant to get a reaction or a change in action out of the other person.

When we compare the way Turtles, Bulldogs, and Foxes attempt to get what they want, it's clear that the Fox uses a particular indirect method of persuading. While Turtles may ask indirect *questions*, such as, "Would you mind scooting over?" when they want another person to make room for them (or they just sit somewhere else because they don't want to ask at all), Bulldogs usually make *direct* statements, such as, "Hey scoot over and make room for me." Foxes, instead, make *indirect statements*, such as, "Looks like you're comfortable taking up the whole couch," to persuade the person to move. If the person doesn't move, he or she looks like the jerk who's comfortable taking up the whole couch. You come away looking clever and you still get a seat on the couch.

Indirect questions also serve the Fox well, such as, "I suppose you're going to work this Saturday, like you usually do?" These loaded questions are veiled statements and are incredibly difficult to answer. To answer "Yes, I'm going to work this Saturday," confirms the Fox's deeper accusation that you prioritize work over your relationship. To answer, "I guess I won't work this Saturday," is to not defend oneself at all against the accusation and hop on the bus for the guilt trip. Not surprisingly, these types of loaded questions usually prompt defensive answers.

There's also a victim mentality that adds power to the Fox's indirect statements and questions. When Jennifer wanted someone to pass her the salad at a dinner I attended, she said, "I guess nobody thinks *I* want any salad." In this way, she indirectly asked for the salad without having to ask a direct question. At the same time, she was able to push off the shame she felt because no one passed her the salad and transfer the shame to the other people at the table for not passing the salad to her. By being a Fox, Jennifer was able to communicate what she wanted, garner sympathy as the victim who had been wronged, and the result? Someone immediately felt ashamed, apologized, and passed her the salad.

When we choose to be a Fox, our passive-aggressive communication feels like a win-win. We get what we want and stay looking good in the process. However, as in the case with Jennifer, shame is often the motivator we use to get what we want, and the long-run consequences in relationships can be devastating.

LET'S TALK 3

1. *Have you ever caught yourself communicating with indirect statements or leading questions like a Fox? If so, what is something you remember saying?*

2. *If you have someone in your life who communicates in this way, how do you typically respond?*

Clever

Like we saw in the salad example, shame is, indeed, a powerful motivator. None of us wants to experience shame. We know others don't want to experience shame, either. So, the Fox is clever, rejecting any shame he or she might be starting to feel and shaming others instead. For example, as a Fox, if we are starting to feel like a friend or loved one might be rejecting us because they haven't called in a while (which makes us ask, "What's wrong with me?" and thus, produces the feeling of shame), we might tell the person on the phone, "Boy, I sure haven't heard from you in a while." Instead of being vulnerable, revealing our emotions, and risking giving the other person the upper hand, we choose to be a Fox to feel more in control. In this clever way, we are able to pass the shame back to the other person as the one at fault, while remaining innocent in our actual words. Truthfully, we haven't heard from the person in a while. However, said with a bite, we can make the other person feel guilty and persuade him or her to call us more often.

The result of this insidious communication style, however, is that the shame we use to motivate the other person destroys the trust in our relationship. The people we want to trust us actually end up fearing us. Afraid of our sharp tongue, loaded statements, and the guilt that lies just around the corner waiting to ambush them, they are careful with what they share and they learn ways to protect their hearts from our arrows.

Children, especially, fall prey to the persuasive cunning of the clever Fox. I have found that if I stomp around the house picking up things, complaining under my breath that, "No one else gives a rip about the mess in this house except me," at least one little boy will feel ashamed and say, "I'll help you, Mommy." However, in shaming my children for not helping around the house instead of stating what I need, I'm creating codependents who feel responsible for my grouchiness. And, as they grow, they will resent the shame I pile on them and learn it is safest to keep their distance. That's good incentive for me to simply ask instead, "Hey, buddy, could you please pick up your shoes and put them away?"

Strategic

There are particular people in my life who I know won't respond to this type of persuasion. They aren't people-pleasers or codependents and they realize I'm actually responsible for my own emotions. More than that, they'll call me on it if I'm acting like a Fox. However, there are other tender souls who respond quickly to being shamed and will do exactly what I want them to do. If I choose to be passive-aggressive in the way I communicate with them, it is a strategic choice; I know it will work. Foxes are excellent readers of people. They know who will respond to their "I-guess-no-one-thinks-I-want-any-salad" method of getting what they want and who won't.

Foxes are also strategic in choosing their words carefully to protect themselves from any unwanted accusations while garnering the response they want to elicit. In answer to "What's wrong?" Foxes strategically turn away while muttering, "Nothing." If the person pries more into what really is wrong, the Fox is adept at shifting the blame to the other party with, "You should know," which helps them come out squeaky clean on the other side.

As a part of their strategic method of communicating, Foxes are masters of body language and facial expression, able to say nice words on the surface while at the same time communicate what they really want with a little pointed emphasis on the right syllable, the shrug of a shoulder, or a raised eyebrow. Therapist Jill Baird calls this, "Sugar-coated poop," meaning it seems really sweet on the outside but it has a yucky pit of anger and bitterness in the middle.

Rachelle knows this type of communication works well on her husband. So, when she's frustrated he hasn't spent enough time at home with her and their two young girls, she turns on her Fox. "Don't worry about me, honey, I'll just stay here with the girls again all day by myself. You go ahead and go golfing with your friends. Have a good time." The words themselves are nice and pretty, but said with the right punch on the right word or two, along with slamming a pillow on the couch, he gets the message loud and clear that she's angry and frustrated and he needs to stay home. I asked her, "So what happens when you do that?" She smiles, "It works. He feels guilty. He stays home."

1. *Evaluate yourself honestly- how often do you use shame to motivate the people in your life?*

2. *Who in your life is most susceptible to this type of motivation?*

3. *What is something you try to motivate him or her to do?*

Influential

The enticing thing about this style of communication is that it works. And it works very well. In this way, the Fox can be extremely influential. People don't want to experience shame, so they cater to the Fox and try to keep him or her happy. If we are the Fox, it's nice to have people desiring to please us and it feels powerful to have found a way to persuade the change we want to see. As Foxes, we wield great influence by our use of shame to motivate the people in our lives.

However, as influential as we feel when we communicate like a Fox, there is still a chicken that is left wounded or dead by our clever methods. What is the chicken? The chicken is the trust in our relationship. If we use manipulative methods to get what we want, someone is being manipulated. And even if he or she can't fully articulate what is happening, the sinking feeling of having been used for someone else's gain is felt. Over time, people learn not to trust us, but to fear us. They begin to associate us with that sinking feeling and they learn to use defense mechanisms to protect their hearts.

If you have ever had a Fox as a parent or sibling or a friend or spouse, you know how manipulated you feel, how it doesn't feel like a win-win. In fact, it feels like a loss every time. Even when you give in to the guilt and cater to their demands, you know it will only keep the Foxes happy for so long and then you're guilted into feeling responsible to please them all over again.

LET'S TALK 5
1. *If you have had a Fox in your life, how has this person's communication style affected your relationship with him/her?*

2. *If you have been a Fox in the past, how do you think your communication style has affected your relationships?*

Why do Foxes communicate this way?

First of all, the methods of a Fox are uniquely indirect, clever, strategic, and influential. Yet, the why behind the what is very similar to the Turtle and the Bulldog. Foxes choose to be Foxes because they found it to be the safest way to attempt to get what they want. When I asked Maria to describe how she communicates with her husband, she explained that since her husband is a Bulldog, if she is too direct with him he will argue back until he wins. But because she still wants to communicate what she wants and needs, she has resorted to being a Fox. Curiously, in her other relationships at work and in her female friendships, Maria finds she rarely chooses passive-aggressive communication strategies.

I asked another colleague, Leslie, about her relationship with her second husband, who is a known Bulldog. I knew Leslie to also be very strong and I could only imagine the fireworks in their marriage. However, Leslie explained that she soon realized she had met her match in direct confrontation with her husband. Upon her discovery that she could never win an argument, she became a Turtle in her relationship with him.

However, I also knew she had been married before and asked her about her first husband. "Oh, he was a Fox," she said. Curious, I asked, "Then, what were you in your first marriage?" She confessed, "I was a Bulldog." That made perfect sense. Her first husband, not wanting to confront her directly, but still wanting to get his needs met, resorted to communicating like a Fox. And Leslie, realizing she couldn't be a Bulldog in her second marriage and still get what she wanted, chose yet another communication style. These stories illustrate the truth that we interact differently in every relationship, employing the communication style we find to be safest and most effective.

Gender

It's possible that your gender has also played a role in you choosing to communicate like a Fox. In the article "Anger Across the Gender Divide,"[1] one researcher suggests that men and women have been socialized to express their anger in different ways. While a boy may have been encouraged to express his anger overtly in fistfights and aggressive language, a girl is typically shamed for that type of aggressive behavior ("It's not ladylike") and may be more likely to use other expressions of anger, such as gossip and loaded comments that can still look socially appropriate on the outside. Thus, some women have developed habits of passive-aggressive communication because it is more socially accepted.

Other research has suggested that women may have learned these communication behaviors to position themselves as superior to other women so as to win the best man, as well as to protect themselves from physical harm.[2] Understandably, some women would also choose less confrontational behaviors in their interactions with men, as men, often being physically stronger, could be perceived as a threat.

However, this is not to say that men are not Foxes. In the face of strong women, like Leslie, some men do choose to communicate like Foxes, especially if they have found that confronting their female counterpart directly poses a risk to getting what they want. Allyson, is a case in point. At first glance, one might guess that she and her husband are both Bulldogs. Outspoken and stubborn, they frequently battle it out verbally in public. Yet, Allyson disclosed to me recently that her husband is actually a Fox who resorts to playing the victim in their relationship to attempt to get what he wants. Not surprisingly, husbands and wives adjust their communication styles to each other to get their needs met in their relationship.

Anger

Underneath the Fox's perceived victimization and "nice" exterior is a wellspring of emotion, including anger and hurt. The Mayo Clinic defines passive-aggressive behavior as,

> "a pattern of indirectly expressing negative feelings instead of openly addressing them...For example, a passive-aggressive person might appear to agree — perhaps even enthusiastically — with another person's request. Rather than complying with the request, however, he or she might express anger or resentment by failing to follow through or missing deadlines."[3]

While Turtles hide and stuff their anger and Bulldogs express their anger directly, Foxes find indirect ways to communicate their anger. Sarcasm is a Fox favorite. I saw a shirt yesterday worn by a teenage girl that read, "I'm Sarcastic Because Violence is Wrong." Truly, the same anger that compels violence also compels us to be sarcastic. And, while slapping someone in the face is not socially appropriate, slapping someone with a comment can actually serve to make the commenter look funny and clever in the eyes of those watching. However, the recipient of the sarcastic comment undoubtedly feels the hurt from the verbal slap.

The anger of the Fox may also be hidden by other means, such as resistance through tardiness, sloppiness, procrastination, or half-hearted involvement. While saying "Okay!" on the outside, the Fox inwardly is not on board. However, afraid of verbally acknowledging their disagreement or unwillingness to cooperate and being rejected, Foxes nonverbally resist in ways that make them feel empowered. If the Fox does verbally acknowledge his or her disagreement, it isn't expressed to the person responsible. Instead, it's expressed to others through gossip or social media channels. Victor explained that since his boss was a Fox who wielded his power by keeping information from the rest of the staff, he felt the only way he could express his resistance was by gossiping and forming a coalition behind his boss' back. In this way, Victor had an outlet for his anger without risking direct retaliation or conflict.

Often, Foxes complain to someone who will risk conflict for them. Like Laura. When a man in front of her stood up during an event, blocking her sight of the stage, Laura complained quietly to her husband, who immediately tapped the man and asked him to sit down. Even though her husband was a Turtle by nature, he acted as the hero for the sake of his wife.

Or Brittany. When a neighbor's dog kept her awake at night, she complained to other neighbors the next day, hoping one of them would confront the dog owner. And thankfully for her, one of them was just as annoyed with the dog and was more than happy to confront the owner.

Hurt

While we may be inclined to point fingers at the Fox for being so conniving, there are also softer emotions underneath the anger we must acknowledge, like hurt. I know, because I have felt it before. One evening, after I had spent a very long day at home with our small children, my husband came home late for dinner. I slapped a dried-out grilled cheese sandwich on a plate and spat out foxily, "Your boss is obviously more important to you than me." He responded, "You know that isn't true." I did know deep down that his boss wasn't more important to him than me, but I was hurt that he had come home late. I wanted him to feel guilty so he wouldn't come home late again and I wanted him to reassure me that he loved me. My hurt and insecurity fueled my loaded comment.

Hurt is a powerful emotion. Yet, expressing the actual hurt requires a vulnerability many of us are not willing to embrace. So, we express it in a way that makes us feel powerful - anger. After years of being married to my husband, I've finally learned that it's safe to express my hurt. And when I feel safe to be vulnerable, I become an Eagle and my Fox is out of sight.

What is the Fox so afraid of?

Showing the hurt and fear we really feel requires taking off the mask of "Strong" and putting on the mask of "Weak." Or, at least we think it looks weak. Sharing our deeper emotions requires vulnerability and feels scary, like we've just unzipped and hung up our bullet-proof vest. What if the other person has no empathy for our hurt or says we deserve it? Or, what if we share something vulnerably and the other person gets angry and rejects us? More hurt and deeper rejection- these are the fears of the Fox.

Connection is ingrained in us as our source for life itself and rejection is a sign we have been disconnected. Loss of connection is one of the greatest fears of the Fox and drives the Fox to hide his or her more vulnerable emotions with an impenetrable front.

Equally strong is the fear of experiencing shame. Bryce had experienced great shame in being rejected by his father when he was a child. Now, as a father with his own son, he was determined not to experience the terrifying shame of rejection or failure ever again. If it started creeping in, he was lightning-fast at shoving it back the other way. When Bryce's son became an adult and expressed his desire that his father apologize for a false accusation, Bryce flipped it back with, "Okay, sure. I'm sorry. And maybe someday I'll hear an apology from you for all the ways you've hurt me."

Owning a mistake is scary when you're a Fox. It means accepting and admitting that you aren't perfect. It means admitting that you're in need of forgiveness and love despite your imperfections. And that feels weak and vulnerable and terrifying. Because what if all of that raw vulnerability results in rejection?

However, when we are the recipients of the shame of the Fox, it can be extremely difficult to see the debilitating fear that is driving this communication style. Foxes have often been wounded by the shame of rejection in past relationships, as in the case with Bryce, and it is precisely this wounding that makes Foxes feel safer when they build protective walls that keep them from having to risk vulnerability. Yet, the redemptive power of empathy is born when we can look deeper than our own hurt to see their fear. Truly, we all have experienced fear and how it drives us to protect ourselves. So, instead of accusing the Fox and responding with the anger that only serves to further entrench the disconnection the Fox fears, we must find the faith to respond with empathy for the fear of the Fox. And, if we are the Fox, we can have compassion on ourselves and commit to address our fear in order to find more life-giving ways of communicating with those around us.

LET'S TALK 6

1. How have anger, hurt, and fear affected your communication choices?

2. If you have a Fox in your life, how can empathy change the way you interact with him or her?

How can faith help the Fox?

As we have explored in this chapter, the Fox is deathly afraid of rejection and the subsequent shame of disconnection. It is precisely this fear that keeps the insecure Fox from risking vulnerability. The cure for our fearful Fox, then, is to first believe we are fully accepted by God. Our sin once created a great gulf between us and our holy God, but because of God's great love for us He bridged that gulf by the death of His Son, Jesus. And when we accept Jesus' death as payment for our sin, our relationship with God the Father is restored and we are fully and completely forgiven and accepted by Him. Our acceptance is the shimmering key that unlocks the door to vulnerability. Once we are secure in our acceptance by our Creator, we can risk revealing our deeper emotions such as hurt or fear to another person. Shame no longer has any power over us. Then, even if that person rejects us for our honesty we rest securely in God's acceptance of us.

Another deep-seated fear for the Fox is experiencing shame. It's because of this fear that the Fox so quickly throws shame the other direction with snide remarks and loaded comments and questions. However, the beauty of the gospel is that Jesus Christ took our shame upon Himself on the cross. He despised it, and He dealt with shame once and for all. I love how John Piper imagines Jesus saying to shame,

"Listen to me, Shame, do you see that joy in front of me? Compared to that, you are less than nothing. You are not worth comparing to that! I despise you. You think you have power. Compared to the joy before me, you have none. Joy. Joy. Joy. That is my power! Not you, Shame. You are worthless. You are powerless...Farewell, Shame. It is finished."[4]

Shame has no power over us anymore because Jesus has conquered it! We no longer have to be afraid of it. And without the fear of shame, we have no need to shove it the other way. When we start to feel shame, we can, instead, admit our imperfections, apologize when we have others, and move on. It's a transformational truth that changes everything.

This morning, I overslept. I didn't get my kids up on time and when my husband came home from working out at 7:30am to take them out for breakfast before school as we had planned, he found me still sound asleep and the house perfectly quiet. I had failed him. As I quickly helped my boys get dressed, I found myself wanting to shame *them* for oversleeping. And in my hard conversation later in the day with my husband, I wanted to shame him for expecting so much of his non-morning-person wife. I wanted to make myself look like a poor victim of his demands and hopefully garner a bit of pity for my exhausted self. Instead, I breathed deep the grace of God and admitted I had mistakenly overslept. That day, I chose not to shame my boys and chose not to shame my husband. It has taken me a long time to realize that Jesus was perfect so I don't have to be. But that realization has made all the difference.

WORDS FROM THE WORD

Read Jonah 1-4

1. *In chapter 1, how was Jonah passive-aggressive in his communication with God?*

2. *What prompted Jonah's transformation in the second chapter of Jonah? How did his communication with God change?*

3. From the rest of the book of Jonah, how do we know that Jonah still struggled with being passive-aggressive?

4. In what ways can you empathize with Jonah?

CREATIVE EXERCISE- "A Picture of Gifts" (for your small group time)

What do you need to be able to communicate in more life-giving ways? Courage? Peace? Wisdom? Faith? In this exercise, your group leader will help you to create frozen and moving pictures to support each other towards your growth as life-giving communicators.

TALK TO GOD

As you close your time together, pray that God would give you:

> *empathy and wisdom as you interact with the Foxes in your life*
>
> *courage to ask for forgiveness when you are wrong*
>
> *grace to accept your imperfections*
>
> *freedom from fear and shame*
>
> *courage to be vulnerable*
>
> *and faith to believe you are fully accepted by God through Jesus Christ.*

SESSION SIX
The Bulldog

Mack glared at the faces all around the conference room table. Fifteen sets of eyes- all directors and managers- looked down and braced themselves. They knew that glare too well—their VP was about to let them have it.

"I tell you we want to increase our market share and no one has any idea this morning how to do that? Last night I saw you at the bar yucking it up, and today, what are you doing? You're all sitting on your hands with nothing to say."

No one said a word. Mack ramped up his volume.

"Every one of you is a coward!" He smacked his hand on the table. "A coward!"

Fifteen sets of eyes continued looking down at the conference table.

"I tell you what—this company is growing. But not one of you are going to last here if you don't start speaking up."

Mack turned and looked directly at Chris, a big man with a goatee and 26 years of experience under his belt. "What about you, Chris?"

Chris looked up from the table at the VP. Mack barked, "Are you a coward, too?"

Known as a high-level leader and an innovative thinker, under Mack's burning gaze even Chris mentally froze. "No, sir."

"Then why are you in here sitting on your hands along with the rest of these cowards? Don't you understand? I don't need cowards; I need leaders! I need people who are willing to offer ideas and be part of the future. If that's not you," Mack pointed to the conference room door, "you can walk out that door right now."

With a family at home to care for, Chris had no intention of walking out any doors. But for the life of him, he was tongue-tied. Any potential solutions to their market share challenge that might have been floating around in his educated, creative mind became scrambled eggs under the edge of Mack's verbal spatula.

"Nothing to say, huh?" Mack pushed his chair back and stood up from the table. He picked up his black notebook. "Then, I'm done here." He walked to the door, but turned back just before he exited, pointed his finger, and made a wide swath around the table. "Let me make myself perfectly clear. None of you will last if you don't start speaking up."

"So, no one ever said anything?" I asked Chris, as we talked by a fire pit one night after a cookout.

"Nope," he said. "I guess everyone was too terrified."

I was curious and dug a little deeper. "What do you think he was afraid of?"

Chris looked surprised at my question. "I don't think he was afraid of anything. He was just trying to motivate us to come up with ways to grow the company."

But I know every positive desire has a flip-side of fear. I offered, "So do you think maybe he was afraid the company wouldn't grow?"

Chris nodded. "Yeah, that's true. He was afraid of that. But barking at all of us didn't work."

"Right, because his communication style shut everyone down. So the room was silent."

Chris laughed, "Yeah, pitch silent. I wasn't about to get my head bitten off."

LET'S TALK 1

How about you? If you wanted to motivate your employees to step it up, given your communication tendencies, how would you have expressed your desire with them at the meeting?

If you typically choose to communicate like a Bulldog, you understand Mack's challenge. Afraid the company is going to stagnate, you have to figure out a way to motivate your managers to engage and offer innovative ideas to grow the company. Telling them in no uncertain terms that they will lose their jobs if they don't engage might seem like a viable option.

Strong and aggressive, the Bulldog's bite is as bad as his bark, and he uses both when he feels provoked or threatened. These tenacious creatures can be either men or women. However, Bulldogs come in varying shades of aggression. And while one person might have a tendency to communicate consistently in aggressive ways, another might choose to communicate aggressively only once in a while or only with certain people, or only when they're defending someone else. Truth is, every one of us has had our "Bulldog" moments.

So, like the Turtle, let's look at this style as a continuum with many points along the line. To find out where you might typically fall on the Bulldog continuum, take the following quiz, made up of 10 questions. And before you say, "I'm not taking this quiz because I've never been and will never be a Bulldog," I dare you to try it, just for fun. Truth be told, even typically passive communicators might have chosen to bare their teeth once in a while given the right situation.

THE BULLDOG QUIZ

Score yourself from 1-5 for each statement, with 1 being Almost Never, and 5 being Almost Always. Then, total your points at the end of the quiz.

1	2	3	4	5
Almost Never	Rarely	Sometimes	Often	Almost Always

_____I have spoken my mind even if I knew it might offend someone else

_____I have said exactly what I was thinking to people in authority

_____If others didn't agree with me, I said what I needed to say to change their minds

_____I have been told I'm intimidating in the way I communicate

_____I typically *tell* people what to do, not *ask* them

_____I have said what I needed to say and didn't worry what other people thought about it

116

_____I have strong opinions and haven't hesitated to express them

_____I haven't been afraid of verbal confrontation

_____I have expressed what I needed even if I knew it could inconvenience someone else

_____I haven't been afraid to say "No" to someone with a strong personality

Total: _____

What Your Score Means
If you scored 10-20, you are rarely a Bulldog. In fact, you rarely choose to use an aggressive communication style to attempt to get what you want. In your experience, you have found one of the other communication styles to be the most effective.

If you scored 20-35, you sometimes choose to be a Bulldog in this situation or relationship; occasionally you use an aggressive communication style to get what you want. In certain instances, you feel like it's safest to take control with your words.

If you scored 35-50, you are a Bulldog in most situations when you feel afraid. This aggressive communication style is your primary fear-based tendency. You have usually found it to be the safest and most effective way to ensure you get what you need and want.

1. What was your score?

2. Are you rarely, sometimes, or usually a Bulldog?

3. Does this ring true for you?

How Does a Bulldog Communicate?

I was walking in my neighborhood one morning when I saw a man taking his short, stout dog with a serious underbite for a walk. "Is that a bulldog?" I asked. He laughed, "Yes, and every bit as stubborn as one, too."

For 350 years, bulldogs were bred to be aggressive for a sport called "bullbaiting." For some reason I can't wrap my mind around, people enjoyed watching an 80lb dog latch his teeth onto the nose of a 1-ton bull and bring him to the ground by "corkscrewing it's own body around its neck and tossing the bull over its own center of gravity."[1] Or the dog was killed by the bull, one of the two. But from what I understand, letting go of the bull's nose and sitting down to work through their relational conflicts was never an option. It was either fight or die.

Thankfully, in 1835, bullbaiting was outlawed and bulldogs were then bred only to do more peaceful things- like herd cattle. Today, the bulldog is associated with strength and loyalty and is the mascot for almost four dozen universities and 250 secondary schools, as well as the unofficial mascot for the US Marines. Historian Marion Sturkey explains that bulldogs "epitomize the fighting spirit of the U.S.

Marines. Tough, muscular, aggressive, fearless, and often arrogant, they are the ultimate canine warriors."[2]

While it may be advantageous to have a bulldog as your mascot, it's a bit more of a challenge to have one as your boss- or your spouse. Yet, because of their decisive communication style, bulldogs can often be found in positions of leadership.

In my work teaching Organizational Communication courses for graduate students, I find that their papers are chock full of tumultuous stories about working for Bulldogs. Similarly, friends and clients are more than willing to share about what it's like being married to a Bulldog or having a Bulldog for a mother or father. However, identifying Bulldogs to interview for this chapter was a bit more tricky. It meant that a Turtle like me who is afraid of conflict had to ask, "I've noticed that you're...quite assertive in the way you communicate. Do you think you might possibly be a 'Bulldog?'" It felt a little like raising my hand to volunteer for WWF, especially if my outspoken coworker retorted, "What makes you think that?" It was much safer to just offer the Communication Style Assessment and let her find out for herself. Then I could follow it up with, "Really? You're a Bulldog!? I had no idea."

When people do acknowledge their typical pattern is a Bulldog, it's generally a cause for laughter, like Alisa who laughed a big laugh that filled the whole café and said, "Oh yes, that's me. I'm definitely a Bulldog!" Or Grant who asked, "Is that the same as foot-in-mouth disease? Yeah, I'm very familiar with it." Or David, who, when I asked if he had any stories about how communicating like a Bulldog had gotten him into trouble, he wrote back, "There is not enough room for me to write!"

This aggressive communication style is marked by 4 characteristics: Direct, Combative, Tenacious and Decisive.

Direct

Remember Doug? The neighbor I asked in Session Four to scoot over a seat at dinner? Doug is known in my neighborhood for being bold and direct. He says exactly what he thinks and is willing to risk offending someone else for the sake of what he believes is right. The quality of being direct is neither good nor bad, but is merely a descriptor of the Bulldog, similar to how the Turtle's quality of being Indirect is neither good nor bad. Being direct is necessary and appropriate in many situations. In fact, as business expert Sylvia Ann Hewlett explains, "being forceful and assertive is a core executive trait."[3]

But being forceful and assertive in the way we communicate can also be seen as aggressive and offensive, as Shana discovered. She wrote in an email to me,

> "When I first started my career, my short and direct emails were offensive to some people outside of our department. My boss received complaints, although I felt I was just trying to be quick and focused. So my boss had a heart-to-heart about adding fluff to my emails and reviewed everything that I emailed to anyone outside our department for a period of time to help me learn how to soften and sweeten my electronic communication."

Another friend, Michelle, explained how her boss asked her to work on being less direct by including it in her development plan. And then she added, "But honestly, the people I had been direct with were incompetent at their jobs

120

and were eventually fired. So I had a good reason to be direct."

Interestingly, when I asked self-professed Bulldogs for an example of when they felt like they had crossed the line, most weren't able to think of a specific example. In fact, when I asked one outspoken man, he thought for a while, but then told me I should talk to his wife because he said she was more of a Bulldog than him. But when I talked with her and described the communication style of the Bulldog, she said, "You mean, my husband?" I said that no, her husband had tagged her as the Bulldog. She laughed and said, "No, he's the Bulldog! But yeah, I do speak my mind. Neither of us have a filter."

Most Bulldogs I spoke with seemed to consider their communication choices appropriate for the situation. It was only when they experienced significant consequences that they realized they had crossed the line. Holly, for instance, was ousted from her volunteer position at a local nonprofit organization because she was perceived as "running over people." Now, she's determined to learn how to tone it down. She calls this, "more clouds," and when she's going into a meeting where she thinks her aggressive style might run over others, she texts me: "Pray for more clouds!"

LET'S TALK 3
Do you prefer to be direct in the way you communicate, especially in tough conversations? Why or why not?

Confrontational

While Turtles hide their heads when conflict approaches, Bulldogs pursue conflict. If something or someone needs confronting, they raise their hands and volunteer to confront it. In the early years of my marriage when my husband and I struggled to see eye-to-eye with extended family members, he would say, "I'm just going to drive over, knock on their door, and have a conversation." And my eyes would get wide as I replied, "You go right ahead. I'll stay here and pray for you." It never ceased to amaze me how he was so unafraid of conflict.

Some Bulldogs may even create conflict just to see what will happen, like Joy, who brings a question to our church supper club that she hopes will create a "lively" discussion, such as, "Would you smoke pot if you lived in a state where it was legal?"

For my colleague, Ken, a middle school teacher, he says he's the only faculty member who's willing to argue with the principal. And he's a self-professed Bulldog, too. He told me the story of when he once was riding to a conference with a group of teachers. He was in the back of the van and the principal was in the front. The principal mentioned that he wanted to implement a new positive behavior program. From the back of the van, Ken pushed back, saying that poor behavior was merely a symptom of a deeper problem. The two of them debated their points vehemently while the teachers in the middle of the van tried to dodge the verbal bullets that went flying through the vehicle.

As it turns out, Ken is the one teacher the principal comes to when he has an idea because he knows Ken will be willing to push back and tell him why it won't work. Now and then, however, Ken's confrontational ways of communicating come back to bite him, like when one of his students dissolved into tears and ran into the bathroom. When she returned, Ken quickly apologized, realizing his aggressive style had hurt her feelings.

Which brings up an important point. While facing conflict boldly can be a positive trait, it can also be a negative trait that makes less aggressive communicators shrink in fear – or dissolve in tears. If you aren't a Bulldog, you are probably thinking of someone you know right now who makes you want to run and hide because of the way he or she communicates. Unfortunately, Bulldogs who consistently create conflict can end up annihilating others and find themselves disconnected from the people they need and love.

LET'S TALK 4
Do you consider yourself confrontational? If so, what motivates you to engage conflict? If you aren't confrontational, how do you feel in a tough conversation with a confrontational person?

Tenacious
Bulldogs in the "sport" of bullbaiting learned to hold on to the death. In the same way, people who communicate in aggressive ways hold onto their preferences and demands and don't feel safe letting go until the other person gives in. If the other person is a family member, this communication style can cause a lot of conflict and even lead to name-calling. One friend of mine was called "uncompromising" by a family

member because of her insistence in what she wanted for an upcoming vacation. Another friend told me how hurt she was when she met a distant relative for the first time. The relative said, "Oh, I hear you're the b---- of the family."

While Bulldogs are called names, like "Bulldog," they also do their share of name-calling to get their point across. Like Mack, who called his employees "cowards," aggressive communicators use extreme means to show how strongly they hold their position. And when they're challenged, they don't back down. They continue escalating the conflict to a breaking point.

I suppose that's why the law profession is known to be chock full of Bulldogs. Tenacity is necessary to fight for the rights of a client. Not surprisingly, one law firm sports a bulldog for their logo and calls themselves "Bulldog Law," explaining that the stubborn canine "symbolizes the tenacious nature of our practice."[4]

In certain situations, we all would like to have a Bulldog in our corner, especially if we are less aggressive communicators. I often pray that my kids will have strong friends who will fight tenaciously for them at school if they're bullied. I pray that my kids will stand up for their friends when it's necessary and appropriate. And I pray that I will have that same boldness. For most of us parents, when it comes to our kids, it's rarely hard to find our inner Bulldog. We might have a hard time standing up for ourselves, but we tenaciously protect our kids, demanding that they be treated well. Mess with one of my sons and you'll see the Bulldog in me.

However, as lawyer John B. Simpson suggests, "there is more to being an effective advocate than simply being adversarial." Simpson asserts that because Bulldogs tend to fight about everything, even things that don't matter, they can end up being "a costly pet to own."[5] Certainly, the catch-phrase "Let it go!" takes on a whole new flavor when applied as advice for the Bulldog. For some, however, they're willing to hang on to the death. Or at least to the point of decision.

LET'S TALK 5
What situations compel you to be tenacious in the way you communicate?

Decisive

"You're fired." It's the phrase that Donald Trump became known for on his TV show "The Apprentice," and it illustrates the fourth characteristic among Bulldog communicators- Decisive. Known for being direct, confrontational, tenacious, and decisive, Trump is polarizing- some people love him and some hate him, evidenced by the tumultuous social aftermath of the 2016 Presidential election. It's no wonder that Trump owned the Georgia Bulldogs for two years.

Sometimes, however, a Bulldog regrets his or her trigger-quick decision making. Vicky is a Physical Therapist who loved her patients but had become increasingly frustrated with her supervisor for giving miniscule raises. She marched up the stairs and into his office. "Brett, this is my 2 week's notice."

However, Brett was a Bulldog, too, and replied, "Actually, you can leave NOW." Miss Decisive had met Mr. Decisive.

Thinking back, Vicky said, "I had really wanted to spend those last 2 weeks with my patients, finishing their treatments, helping them set goals, and letting them know I was leaving. I had no idea my boss would one-up me by making me leave right then. If I could go back, I would do it differently."

LET'S TALK 6
If you're decisive, when have your decisive ways come back to bite you?

Why does the Bulldog communicate this way?

For those of us who are Turtles, we are baffled by Bulldogs. Why do they communicate in such direct, confrontational, tenacious and decisive ways? Don't they want peace and harmony like we do? When I asked Joy why she seemed to like conflict, she said enthusiastically, "Because it's entertaining! Without any conflict, it's just plain boring. Makes me want to scratch my eyes out." And when I asked Ken what made him want to argue with the principal while they rode in the van on the way to the conference, he said it was his way of working out his doubts, listening to the principal's rebuttals to his reservations, and deciding whether or not he wanted to get on board with the program. And in the end, he did.

Bulldogs also communicate in direct ways because they see their style as being much more efficient. Rick said he didn't have time to be anything but direct. Kaylee told me, "It's just so much faster to say what I want without the fluff." Her Bulldog friend, Lila, chimed in, "Adding fluff just takes so much extra thought and energy."

The truth is, Bulldogs have found that being aggressive is the safest way to get what they need and want. However, there are other factors that may influence a more aggressive communication style. These include culture, family of origin, gender, and circumstances.

Culture

For some Bulldogs, their aggressive communication style is their way of surviving in their culture- or the way they think they need to communicate to survive. One of my Indian friends is a case in point. When I talked with him about his communication style, he explained to me that he learned at a young age that if he didn't communicate like a Bulldog in his country, no one would hear him. In fact, he said he would have been figuratively "eaten alive." In order to survive, he learned to be aggressive. Eat or be eaten. Now living in America, he still communicates in aggressive ways. As a businessman, that works well for him since America is considered to be a "direct culture" in which it's appropriate in business to tell others exactly what you need from them.[6]

Communication researchers label countries "indirect" or "direct," with Arab countries and Asia falling under the "indirect" label, and America and Germany categorized as "direct." Indirect cultures rely on many other cues other than words to decipher meaning and so are considered "high-context" cultures. Direct cultures, or "low-context" cultures, rely heavily on the words themselves to convey and decipher meaning.[7] Interesting to me, in light of my aggressive Indian friend, is that researchers categorize India as a more indirect, high-context culture, although some assert that that India today is moving closer to becoming a low-context culture, similar to America.[8] Obviously, one can't assume that if a person is from a particular culture, he or she will communicate directly or indirectly, according to your cultural definitions of those terms. Variations in style abound no matter where you were raised, and, in fact, your style may be a reaction to your culture. For me, being raised in a direct culture has made me shy away from direct communication, while my Indian friend, raised in a more indirect culture, has clearly decided that direct communication is the best way to get his needs met.

Even in the U.S. however, where direct communication is often expected, there are certain areas of the country where an indirect style is more accepted, such as the South. Take, for instance, the southern term, "Bless your heart." It sounds really sweet, but said to a disorganized teen who keeps losing his keys might actually mean, "You would lose your head if it weren't attached to your neck." Indeed, Bulldogs in the deep south like Mississippi might have a hard time figuring out how to be acceptably direct. They may even decide communicating like a Fox is safer. However, in a northeastern state like New Jersey, a Bulldog might just cut to the chase with, "Forget about it- you're an idiot."

Your Family

Many self-reported Bulldogs I interviewed traced their communication style choices back to the influence of their family of origin. Like Gretchen. Gretchen grew up in a family of Turtles and said she "saw how they never got anything done." When she left home, she decided she didn't want to live that way. She wanted to "get things done." So she decided to start speaking her mind. "Life is too short not to say what I think," she said.

Your family of origin is the first "culture" you experience, with its own set of cultural norms and rules. Some of us learned in our families that speaking up got us what we wanted. Others of us learned that speaking up made us a target for well-aimed arrows. But when you and your siblings grow up in the same house and come out with very different communication styles, it proves that much more than the influence of your family is at work in your choices.

Gender

Gender may also play a part in whether or not you choose to communicate like a Bulldog. In the 1970's, social scientist Virginia Schein studied the connection between gender stereotypes and management characteristics. She found that masculine attributes, like aggressiveness and competitiveness, are considered to be more suitable for leadership, while feminine traits, such as being less analytical and taking care of others, are considered to be more suitable for serving.[9] Which explains why men, whose communication style is often characterized by more masculine attributes, are often promoted to leadership positions.

However, as Hewlett found in her research, women who adopt masculine traits, such as communicating aggressively, are often punished for it and eventually learn to be less direct,[10] like Shana and Michelle, who I mentioned earlier in this chapter. My colleague, Ben, however, had been told at work that he was too reticent and needed to be more aggressive if he wanted to be successful. Clearly, gender plays a key role in socially acceptable methods of relating to others. If you are affirmed and rewarded for being aggressive in the way you communicate, you will probably continue to choose to be direct, confrontational, tenacious, and decisive. And, if you are continually reprimanded for being too direct, even if it is your natural bent, you may try to keep the traits of your Bulldog under wraps.

Circumstances

For some of us, we may tend to be Turtles or Foxes most of the time in the way we communicate when we are afraid, but there may be relationships or circumstances that bring out the aggression in us. One friend of mine whose daughter has special needs invited the other parents in her neighborhood to her house and then told them in no uncertain terms that their kids had better stop bullying her daughter or she would take matters into her own hands.

Perceived hurt may also compel us to communicate in aggressive ways. Like Dave. Dave had chosen to communicate like a Turtle all his life, shrinking from confrontation and keeping any negative feelings to himself. But when he suddenly believed he had been undercut by his brothers out of the proceeds from the sale of a family business, he began sending blistering emails, making demands and accusations, and finally cutting himself off from them entirely. He shocked everyone by suddenly becoming direct, confrontational, tenacious and decisive.

Circumstances around your mode of communication may also influence your style. Research has shown that people are often much more bold on texting, email and social media than they may be in face-to-face situations. Under the cover of digits on a screen, the "disinhibition effect" comes into play as the fear of immediate face-to-face consequences is mitigated.[11]

What elements of your culture, family of origin, gender, and circumstances have influenced you in the past to communicate at times like a Bulldog?

What's the Bulldog so afraid of?

But why? Why would Dave suddenly choose to communicate that way? At the outset, we could say he was trying to get his needs met. Or he was attempting to get what he wanted. Perhaps he tried the agreeable Turtle approach the first time around, but it didn't get him anywhere. And then he tried to be clever like a Fox, but it didn't work either. So he ramped it up.

But let's dig down a little deeper. As I wrote in the beginning of this chapter, every positive desire has a flip side of fear. So what was Dave afraid of? If his positive desire was to get his needs met, the flip-side was being afraid of *not* getting his needs met. He was afraid of losing out on something he believed was rightfully his and wanted it badly enough to try a more aggressive strategy.

At a coffee shop recently, Mindi confessed that her marriage was not in a good place. "I ask my husband to tell me what he's thinking, but he says I'm not a safe place for him. So he keeps it to himself."

I asked, "What do you think you're doing that makes him feel like you aren't safe?"

"I guess I get really yell-y," she said, "And then he just shuts down."

Mindi admits to her tendency to communicate like a Bulldog. At work, she's been known to fire off aggressive emails to clients and has suffered their wrath in return. Now, she's experiencing the consequences of her communication style in her marriage. Mindi desperately wants to connect with her husband, but demanding it doesn't seem to be working.

Your deep drive to connect with the people around you is rooted in your first weeks and months of life- you had to stay connected to your mother to get your needs met. As an adult, you bring that same construct into your relationships, knowing that you need to stay connected to others in order to get your needs met.

Take Mack, for instance, the business leader in the beginning of this chapter. I highly doubt he would recognize his own need for connection and how it motivated his demand that his managers cough up innovative ideas. But what he was essentially saying to them through all his barking, was "Stay connected to me! Stay connected to my vision to grow this company! Don't you dare disconnect from me! If you disconnect from me, I disconnect from you!" To take the connection concept a little further, if his company goes downhill, what will happen to his connection with other businessmen in the community? Will he be rejected from among their ranks? What will happen to his family who may be depending on him to provide for them? Will they lose respect and disconnect from him?

Losing connection brings with it the visceral experience we all try to avoid- shame. Like the heavy blanket the dentist lays across your chest before taking an x-ray, shame feels heavy. Shame tells you, not that you merely *made* a mistake, but that you *are* a mistake. To avoid that feeling, much like the Fox, Bulldogs push the shame off onto other people with the way they communicate. Yet, unlike the Fox, they use *direct* words to try to control a person or situation. Dave, afraid of experiencing the shame of financial distress, shamed his brothers for undercutting him. Mindi, afraid of experiencing the shame of disconnection to her husband, has admitted to shaming him for not opening up. And Mack, afraid of experiencing the shame of a failed business, shamed his employees for not being innovative. The problem is, by trying to control others with shame, Bulldogs ultimately sabotage what they want- connection.

Connection is life. And every one of us is afraid of experiencing shame and not getting our needs met. We just use different methods to deal with our fear. The Turtle uses no words, the Fox uses manipulative words, and the Bulldog uses demanding words. By being direct, confrontational, tenacious and decisive, the Bulldog deflects shame, demanding that others meet his or her needs. When others refuse, the Bulldog first tries barking louder and biting harder. And if that doesn't work, he or she might decide to try a different strategy altogether.

How can faith help the Bulldog?

For the Bulldog, releasing control by choosing to use less forceful words can be terrifying. "What if they don't give me what I need or do what I want them to do?" one Bulldog friend asked. The key for our inner Bulldog to conquer this fear is to learn to trust.

What is it exactly that the Bulldog can trust? We can trust that God is in control. He is the only One who can change the heart of the other person and ultimately the only One who can meet our deepest needs for value and connection. In Job 38:34, we read God's question to Job, "Can you send forth lightnings, that they may go and say to you, 'Here we are'?" God controls the lightning, and when he wants it to rain, He tilts "the waterskins of the heavens" (38:37b). He commands the morning (38:12), gives the horse his might (39:19a), and directs the heart of a king: "The king's heart is like channels of water in the hand of the Lord; He turns it wherever He wishes" (Prov. 21:1). When we know that God is ultimately in charge, it gives us the faith to let go of our need to control and to speak in life-giving ways to the people around us.

We also trust that God will meet our needs. While it is our responsibility to communicate what we need, demanding what we need with forceful words often causes others to shrink back from us. They may give us what we need in the short run, but our aggressive communication style sabotages the ultimate connection we so desire in the long run. As Paul told the Philippian church in 4:19, "...my God will supply all your needs according to his riches in glory in Christ Jesus." When you trust that God will meet your needs, it gives you the freedom to choose life-giving words from a place of faith instead of choosing controlling words from a place of fear.

Jim had been a no nonsense upper-level manager at his workplace. Known for his red-hot temper, he was quick to shame an employee for a mistake, yell at another to get a point across, and fire anyone who crossed him. Not surprisingly, people were afraid of him and his department had the highest turnover of any department at his company. However, he revealed to me with tears that after he realized his deep value to His Creator and put his faith in Jesus Christ, everything changed. He now had an anchor for his desperate soul. Over time, his communication became life-giving. He had more patience and gave his employees respect by really listening to them during difficult conversations. Since he had experienced being valued by God, he was able to speak value to others, knowing they were also valued by God. And, once they felt heard and valued, his team members no longer wanted to leave. Today, he hasn't had an employee leave his department in 8 years.

WORDS FROM THE WORD

Read Mark 8:32 and 9:5.

1. *In each of these passages, what evidence can you find that Peter communicated too aggressively?*

2. *What do you think motivates Peter's communication in Mark 8:32?*

3. *What do you think motivates Peter's communication in Mark 9:5?*

Now read Acts 2:1-41

4. In this passage, how is Peter's communication different from the passages in Mark? What is the response from the people?

5. What events did Peter experience between Mark 9 and Acts 2 that may have influenced his transformation? What evidence can you find that they influenced him?

Like Peter, God is in the process of growing and maturing your communication style. In Philippians 1:6, we read, "...He who began a good work in you will perfect it until the day of Christ Jesus." Undoubtedly, we will all still have moments in which we revert to fear and use controlling words with the people around us. The key is to recognize our fear and consciously make the decision to trust the Lord to meet our needs, to trust Him to change the heart of the other person, and to allow the Holy Spirit to speak value through us. When we make that conscious decision to trust, that's when we'll partner with God to truly "say it brave" and see our words transformed into life-giving words.

LET'S TALK 8

In what relationship or situation is God asking you let go, trusting that He is ultimately in control?

CREATIVE EXERCISE- OUTSIDE/INSIDE (during your small group time)

Create a posture that represents a "Bulldog" in your mind. Then, create a posture that represents how you feel when you are communicating with a Bulldog. During your small group time, your small group leader will guide you in discovering the difference between what we show others on the outside and what we feel on the inside. You will have an opportunity to share your postures and interact with the postures of others.

TALK TO GOD

As you close your time together...

> *pray that you would have empathy for the Bulldogs in your life*

> *confess your desire to control others in the way you communicate*

> *ask God to give you the faith to trust Him in your specific situations and relationships*

> *pray for self-awareness to discern if you are communicating from fear or faith*

> *and ask God to transform your communication so that, like Peter experienced, people will be drawn to Jesus.*

SESSION SEVEN
The Eagle

I heard a knock at my office door. "Come in!" I said. My boss, Mickey, entered. I scanned his face. He seemed troubled. "Heidi, can I talk with you for a minute?"

"Sure." I closed my laptop and pushed myself back from my desk. As the creative director for a large church, I was in the middle of a stressful rehearsal schedule for our annual Christmas musical. But I usually enjoyed my conversations with Mickey and didn't mind his interruption.

He was acting a little differently than normal, however. Perhaps not quite as happy or... light as usual. And, he wasn't carrying anything- no clipboard, no notes, so I knew he wasn't asking me to go over something or to revisit the agenda from our creative planning meeting earlier that morning.

Then, he did something even more curious. He crossed to the left side of my desk and got down on his knees, his arms resting on the desk surface.

"Uh-oh," I thought. Whatever this was about, it was serious. I swiveled my chair towards him. Since he was on his knees, he was nearly at my eye level.

"Heidi, I really appreciate the work you're doing on the musical."

"Thanks," I responded, a bit skeptically.

"How do you think rehearsals are going?" he asked.

I nodded, "Good! I think it's all coming along really well."

He looked down at the desk, then back up at me, and said calmly. "So, I need to talk with you about the rehearsal schedule. I'm hearing that people feel like it's too much. You know, because they need to spend time with their families."

A zillion defenses rushed through my mind, like, "Compared to a real theater this rehearsal schedule is nothin'!" and "Do you want a high quality production, or not?" But there he was, on his knees in front of me, looking straight into my eyes. Not threatening, just wanting to bring an issue to my attention. I took a deep breath and tried to match his humility and maturity.

"I can understand that. I just want the musical to be really good."

He nodded, "And that's what makes you good at what you do. I know you want it to be good. I've been there. And you know what? It will be good."

His encouragement and empathy softened me. Then, he asked, "So, what could we do to help the cast not feel so overworked?"

I appreciated him asking for my opinion. He clearly valued my voice and believed I could help find the solution; we were on the same team. I sighed, "Well, I could go back and look at the rehearsal schedule and see if I could consolidate a few of them."

I dug deep to find some empathy, too. "I know they're just volunteers." I had seen the little girl who came with her dad every week to rehearsal. She sat in a seat in the auditorium, coloring, while he was on stage. I wasn't married at the time and didn't have any kids, but I knew what it was like to want to spend time with my dad. I could rework the schedule.

Mickey nodded. "Thanks, Heidi. I appreciate what you do." And with that, he got up off his knees and left my office.

That conversation took place over 20 years ago, but I can still picture it vividly today. In that conversation, if I try to peg Mickey as a Turtle, a Fox, or a Bulldog, I can't. Despite the fact that I hadn't given him much reason to trust me on a human level, he chose to speak the truth in a way that preserved his connection with me. And in the end, while I got the message about the changes I needed to make, I still felt heard, cared for, and valued.

LET'S TALK 1

1. How might a Turtle, a Fox, and a Bulldog have communicated the same information?

2. What strikes you most about the way Mickey communicated?

If you've ever been in Mickey's shoes, you know the fear you feel when volunteers start complaining about being overworked. If they are unhappy enough, they'll quit. At the same time, you know how tricky it can be to confront someone who recoils under criticism, like me. Your job is to assess the situation and figure out the most non-threatening way to express your concerns to your employee.

It isn't easy to be an Eagle. Or, we could say, it isn't easy to "Speak Eagle." Our default, knee-jerk reactions like hiding, sniding, or attacking feel so natural and so much safer- as if we have a chance at some control over an out-of-control situation. However, I'll bet there have been many times in your past when you did communicate like an Eagle. Take the following assessment to find out.

THE EAGLE QUIZ

As with the previous quizzes, answer each question honestly with a number between 1 and 5, with 1 being Almost Never and 5 being Almost Always.

1	2	3	4	5
Almost Never	Rarely	Sometimes	Often	Almost Always

_____ I have respectfully defended someone who was being hurt

_____I have used my words and actions to affirm the value of the people around me

_____I have been wise in my communication for the benefit of another person or group of people

_____When someone has hurt me, I have respectfully expressed my hurt

_____I have been able to release my need to change another person with my words or actions

_____ I have respectfully shared my honest feelings

_____When I have been made aware that I hurt someone,
I have humbly apologized

_____ I have respectfully asked someone for what I needed

_____When someone has shared his or her feelings with me,
I have responded with empathy

_____ I have respectfully defended myself when I was being
hurt

Total: _____

What Your Score Means

If you scored 10-20, you have rarely chosen to "speak Eagle."
Up to this point in your life, you have not seen this
communication style as an effective way to get what you
want. However, since we become Eagles one trusting choice
at a time, there is hope- you are an Eagle in the making.

If you scored 20-35, you sometimes have chosen to speak
Eagle; occasionally you have used this style to attempt to get
what you want. While you may sometimes default to your
natural tendencies, the fact that you do speak Eagle, even
once in a while, should encourage you.

If you scored 35-50, you usually choose to speak Eagle; this
life-giving communication style is your style of choice. You
are able to communicate in a way that allows you to protect
yourself and others, yet expresses freedom and value to those
around you.

Speaking Eagle demands a great deal of intentionality. It urges that "the heart of the righteous ponders how to answer" (Proverbs 15:28) and requires us to conquer our fears of being rejected, to find the courage to be vulnerable, and to release our desire to force another person to change.

LET'S TALK 2
1. *What was your score?*

2. *According to the quiz, do you "speak Eagle" rarely, sometimes, or usually?*

3. *Does this ring true for you?*

Why an Eagle?
Three unique features of the eagle make it an excellent metaphor for a good communicator: eagles have powerful vision, they are loyal partners, and they are able to soar.

Powerful Vision
Eagles have incredible vision, seeing four to five times farther than we do. They also have the ability to magnify distant images and perceive colors more vividly than we do.

"If you swapped your eyes for an eagle's, you could see an ant crawling on the ground from the roof of a 10-story building. You could make out the expressions on basketball players' faces from the worst seats in the arena. Objects directly in your line of sight would appear magnified, and everything would be brilliantly colored, rendered in an inconceivable array of shades."[1]

When we speak Eagle, we also have incredible vision, seeing our own communication through the lens of self-awareness as well as seeing into the needs and fears of others. Like the magnification skill of the eagle, Eagle communicators are able to visualize the future and make choices now in interactions that help them move toward health and connection.

Loyal Partner

The second compelling feature of eagles is that they partner for life.[2] This means they choose one mate, work together to build their nest, and remain loyal to their mate their entire lives. As believers, we have chosen to partner with God for life, work together to build the kingdom of God, and remain faithful to Him throughout our lives. As we walk hand-in-hand with Jesus, we don't just communicate in healthy ways for a better experience here on earth; we know that there are spiritual implications for every word we speak. Others may choose to turn away from God or turn toward Him, motivated by our words and actions. And we ourselves may be drawn in dependence to God as we make communication choices in our difficult conversations that require us to trust Him.

However, we know God is the one who truly does the spiritual work in each of us. In *Experiencing God*, authors Blackaby and King explain that God is always at work.[3] And He invites each of us to join Him in the work He is doing. When we use our eagle vision to see where God is at work to draw us and others to Himself in dependence, we then can respond by joining God, making choices that grow our faith and the faith of those around us.

Ability to Soar

Partnering with God also means we have another Helper- the Holy Spirit. He fills us with His power as we rest in our relationship with the Father through Jesus Christ. While most birds flap their wings to fly, the eagle uses the power of the wind to soar instead.[4] Soaring is a much more efficient use of the eagle's energy, who spends a great deal of time in the air waiting patiently, scanning the ground and water for potential food to appear.

For us, it can't be only about working harder in our own strength to be good communicators, especially in our difficult conversations. It must be about relying on God's strength as He works in us and through us. And, as the Holy Spirit fills us, we can soar on faith, speaking words of life and waiting patiently for Him to do His work in the heart and life of the other person. "They that wait on the Lord will renew their strength, they will mount up with wings like eagles; they will walk and not be weary, they will run and not faint. Teach us, Lord, to wait" (Is. 40:31).

If you've ever seen an eagle soaring, you know the beauty of the outstretched wings, the effortless flight. And, if you've ever been the recipient of the words and actions of an Eagle communicator, you know the connection, safety, and freedom you feel in his or her presence.

LET'S TALK 3

1. *Which characteristic of the Eagle is the most striking to you? Why?*

2. *Which characteristic of the Eagle do you feel like you need the most right now in the way you communicate? Why?*

How does an Eagle communicate?

When you communicate in life-giving ways, you become an Eagle. And while perfection isn't possible this side of heaven, every one of us can have Eagle moments. We've looked at three striking qualities of the eagle in nature. Now let's look at four characteristics that make up the Eagle communicator: Trusting, Discerning, Empathetic, and Forward-thinking.

Trusting

While the Turtle, the Fox, and the Bulldog are motivated by fear (especially fear of rejection, the loss of connection and control, and the resulting shame), the Eagle is motivated by trust. From a human perspective, we cannot always trust the people around us. Your score on Part II of the Assessment in Session 3 may have made that clear for particular relationships. So, our trust can't be rooted in the other person. It must be rooted in God. Trusting God that you are secure in His love as your Acceptance-Giver, that He is in control as the Heart-Changer, and that He has freed you from fear as your Shame-Taker (see Session 2) can give you extraordinary courage to speak the truth in love. If our trust is rooted in God, then our decision to speak Eagle isn't determined by the people or our ability to trust them.

It isn't an accident that both speaking the truth and speaking love are packed into that dynamite 5-word phrase, "speaking the truth in love" from Paul's letter to the Ephesians (4:14-15): "...we are no longer to be children...but speaking the truth in love, we are to grow up in all aspects into Him..." For some of us, speaking the truth feels scary when you'd rather just speak love, and for others of us speaking love feels scary when you'd rather just speak truth. But, resting securely in faith and your ultimate acceptance by God, you can speak the truth and even be vulnerable in sharing your heart. And resting securely in faith and God's ultimate sovereignty, you are able to speak love, offering freedom to the other person to change - or not change. Specifically, we can trust God with our values, our longing, and our purpose.

Values

When you are an Eagle, you trust that your values are God's values. Knowing His Word is essential to knowing what He values. Recently, I was given the assignment for a leadership group to study the gospel of John to identify Jesus's values. The top value I identified was "life." Jesus values life. That's why he healed the sick and cast out demons and preached about how to have eternal life. Since God values life, you can trust that He will give you the courage to defend someone who is being hurt, to affirm the value of those around you, and to defend yourself when necessary.

Setting boundaries to protect your heart and life, even as you speak freedom to the other person, is to partner with God in the work He is doing to value life- your life. Shift your perspective so that the boundaries you set for yourself and your family are not drawn because you are afraid but because you value your life and heart and long for it to be treasured.

At a Heart Perception Project lunch in Seattle with my friend Kellie's colleagues, I found myself sitting in a group of strong Pro-Choice supporters. They were incredulous that, as a woman with a Ph.D., I would not support the rights of women to "control their own bodies." The woman next to me asked, "Why would you not stand up for women's rights?"

I felt my heart start to race as if I was being threatened. I took a breath and then said, "Just so you know, I'm feeling myself getting really anxious right now. Could you please phrase your question as a curious question?"

She was surprised and visibly backed down. "Oh! I'm sorry. Sure." She thought a moment and then asked, "Okay, what is it about the abortion issue that makes you feel so strongly?"

I thanked her for her truly curious question and then explained that I see unborn children as a marginalized people group who don't have a voice. I feel passionate about being a voice that says their lives have value. The woman nodded thoughtfully. She and the others said they could empathize with my passion to stand up for the lives of a people group I consider "marginalized," something she does often with other marginalized groups of people.

However, the woman on the other side of me said, "I'm feeling shame right now because I had an abortion."

Because I also value her life, and God values her life, I put my hand on her arm. "I can imagine that was a very hard decision for you."

Her eyes filled with tears. She brushed them away and shook her head. "But I dealt with the shame of it a long time ago."

Without Christ, we only have human means to deal with the shame we experience. And those means are poorly ineffective. While shame from the enemy will spiral us down to death, godly shame will spiral us up to life. I believe God can actually use shame to compel us to repent and to run to His embrace. And once we repent, our shame is buried in the ocean of His grace. As my friend and writer Gigi McMurray once told me, "His grace fuels even the slightest turn of the soul towards Him." In that moment, I discerned that I was to express empathy for the woman's pain and value for her life. I pray that one day she will experience freedom from the shame that still stabs her heart.

When you are anticipating a difficult conversation, ask yourself, "In this situation, what does God value?" Spend time in His Word to confirm that this is what God values. Ask Him to speak His values through you.

Longing

It's a distinction that changes everything when we are motivated in our tough conversations by *longing* instead of fear. In their book, *Bold Love*, authors Allender and Longman completely turned my world upside-down with their suggestion that we set boundaries not out of our fear of being hurt but out of our longing for beauty. They write, "Beauty borrows its light from the glory of God...When beauty is defiled or tarnished, there is a loss, and anger, a sorrow—a desire to see it put right."[5] When we have a difficult conversation in which we need to communicate a boundary to someone who is hurting us, we do so because we value the beauty of healthy relationships and the beauty of our own hearts. And we know God values these things as well.

Offering another person the freedom to change (or not change) can be motivated by longing, trusting that your longings for beauty and life have been written on your heart by your Heavenly Father. While you might not use the phrase, "I long for this for you," directly, your longing for the good instead of your fear of the bad underlies the words you choose to use. For example, if your brother smokes and you know it's killing him, a tough conversation with him can be rooted in your value of his life. So, instead of trying to persuade him with fear and shame by saying, "You're killing yourself, bro; you've got to stop smoking," you can express your heart, instead, with, "Hey, bro, I love you. I want you to live for a long time. Please stop smoking."

Setting a boundary with your brother might mean you tell him he has the freedom to keep smoking, but that if he does so he will need to finish his cigarette before visiting with your children. However, instead of lacing the consequences with shame by saying, "If you don't stop smoking, I won't let my kids be around you," you can phrase it positively by saying, "I really value your relationship with my kids. Whenever you aren't smoking you are welcome to visit with them." You might honestly be afraid of the consequences of second-hand smoke, but you choose not to communicate from that fear but from your longing for your brother's health and your relationship with him instead.

In 2 Peter 3:9, we read that God is patient with us, not wanting "any to perish, but longing for all to come to repentance." He doesn't force us, but says that He stands "at the door" and knocks (Rev. 3:20) and offers us the choice to open the door. As one of God's values is freedom, when we communicate from a place of longing, offering the freedom to change or not change, then we are able to let go and trust God to do His work.

Do you hear the difference it makes to communicate from a place of longing instead of fear? Fear is often laced with anger and shame and typically spurs defensiveness and fear-based communication from the other person. Longing reveals our softer emotions, such as loneliness, and may pave the way to also bring out the softer emotions in the one we are confronting.

Purpose

Finally, when you're an Eagle, you also trust that this interaction has a divine purpose- it's essential for your own health and growth, for the health and growth of the other person, and perhaps even for a larger group of people. This confidence gives you the courage to apologize, to confront when necessary and to be vulnerable when appropriate. When I asked Sandy to show me a posture that represented how she felt about tough conversations, she leaned forward in her chair, resting her forearms on her thighs, palms turned upwards. Her expression communicated an eagerness to connect. I asked her to explain what she was feeling. She said, "I'm confident because I know I'm right where I'm supposed to be; God has led me here." Sandy spoke as an Eagle.

The purpose of our tough conversations is not to change each other but to deepen our dependence on Christ so that He can change us both. God has created you with your unique personality, your abilities and longings, and put you in this situation and relationship for such a time as this. Trusting that He has led you here and He will speak to you and through you by the power of the Holy Spirit allows you to rest in Him, believing that He will do His work in you and in the lives of those around you.

LET'S TALK 4
What is the most challenging part of trusting God in your difficult conversations?

Trusting does not mean we can trust that others will make good decisions, change in any way, or even respond positively to our initiation. However, from what we have learned about communication styles up to this point, one perception we can trust is that their negative or hurtful words are usually rooted in fear, not in hate or malice. This knowledge allows us to believe the best about them, to empathize with their fear, and to discern the most life-giving way to respond.

Discerning

While my boss, Mickey, did get on his knees next to my desk for the conversation I described at the beginning of this chapter, he never did it again. And whether his action was spontaneous or premeditated, I'm not sure. In fact, I asked him recently about that interaction and he didn't remember it at all. What I do know is that he trusted that our conversation was necessary and he discerned that I would be most receptive if he delivered the information while on his knees next to my desk. He was right. Had he been standing up, lording his authority over me while I was sitting down, I probably would have immediately become defensive. Had he even been sitting in a chair across from my desk, it might have felt formal and detached with the desk between us. On his knees next to my desk, however, he showed me that he was on my team and he gave me a glimpse into the humility of his heart.

Every situation and relationship poses an opportunity for us to ask God for wise judgment in how to approach a risky interaction. We know from James 1:5 that if we need wisdom we only have to ask God in faith and He will give it generously.

Eagles use their discernment to first assess their safety, the time, and the location. And then the Eagle considers guidelines from the Word, the prompting of the Holy Spirit, and selects the wisest communication style for the situation.

Safety

If there is a possibility the other person will respond in a hostile manner to what you need to say, invite another person to accompany you. Inviting a friend or colleague to be present can help give you peace of mind, as well as provide accountability for you and the other person to use self-control in the conversation.

Time of day

Also, consider the time of day and choose a time when neither of you are hungry or tired, if possible. Many a "hangry" conversation could have been avoided had we only chosen a different time of day. Thoughtfully consider, as well, when the other person might be the least stressed or anxious. Nighttime conversations are especially problematic, as researchers have found that people generally feel more negative at night than in the morning.[6]

Location

Along with considerations of your safety and the time of day, avoid territorialism by choosing a neutral location. In our own territories, we might be less apt to stand down or consider another viewpoint. However, if we meet in a neutral location, we have a better chance of objectively using our rational minds to ask each other curious questions, listen attentively, and consider creative ways to more forward.

Take, for example, your concern for your brother who smokes. If you meet with him in his home to express your concern while he is enveloped in his favorite recliner with his favorite ashtray on the end table next to him, he may feel very emotionally connected to his tradition of smoking and fight you to keep it. On the other hand, if you meet with him in your home where everything is placed where you want it, your way, he might also be disinclined to consider your point of view, and you might have a hard time truly hearing his viewpoint, as well. Having the conversation in a neutral location, then, like a coffee shop or a park bench, allows you to come together, independent of your personal props, to find resolution like teammates who are on the same team playing for a common goal.

We also need look to the Word of God and the Holy Spirit to help us be discerning communicators.

The Word

As we are grounded in faith, we know our freedom has limits because we are guided by the Word of God. The Word is chock-full of godly advice for how to be a redemptive communicator as well as the pitfalls of destructive communication.

Look up the following verses and write down what you learn about godly communication:

James 3:6-11

Exodus 20:7

Ephesians 4:29

I Thessalonians 5:11

Matthew 12:34

The Holy Spirit

Discernment is the key to knowing what to say, when to say it, where to say it, and how to say it. Feels a little overwhelming, doesn't it? Take heart. Since communication is a dynamic process filled with emotion and unpredictable responses, it's impossible to have it all figured out before we walk into a difficult conversation. Our only hope is to prepare as well as we can and ask the Holy Spirit to fill us and give us the discernment we need in the moment. The words of Jesus are reassuring when He encouraged the disciples, "But when they hand you over, do not worry about how or what you are to say; for it will be given you in that hour what you are to say" (Matthew 10:19).

Finally, we need wisdom to discern the communication style of the other person and adapt our own style accordingly for that relationship and the situation.

Communication styles

Mickey had worked with me long enough to know my aversion to conflict. So, he approached me in a way that assured he had no intention of fighting- or rejecting me. As you consider the person with whom you need to talk, think about his or her communication tendencies. Then, ask yourself, what might he or she be afraid of? Remember, we are all afraid of many things- especially the shame of failure, rejection, loss of control, and loss of connection. What particular fear might your discussion trigger in this person?

As you prepare your heart, ask God to give you discernment to understand the heart of the other person so that you can voice your concerns in a way that acknowledges and even diffuses the underlying fears. If diffusion isn't possible and you know the information you have to deliver will pour fuel on the shame the person already feels, pray for discernment in how you can point that person to God, the only one who can truly deliver us from our fear of experiencing shame.

LET'S TALK 5

1. *If you are anticipating a difficult conversation in the near future, what is the conversation about and what do you think the other person might be afraid of?*

2. *What might you be able to say or do to help alleviate the other person's fear?*

3. In Philippians 1:9-11 in your Bible, circle the word *"discernment."* According to this verse, what are some of the results of discernment?

"Speaking Eagle" means speaking the truth in love, but that doesn't necessarily mean always speaking meekly. It means bravely choosing to communicate from a place of trust instead of fear. Sometimes you will assess the situation and discern that it's time for you to stand on faith courageously-speaking firmly and even raising your voice when necessary to protect yourself and others. Or, you may intentionally choose to be strategic, employing a clever mode "with the pure desire of seeing God's glory reign supreme... outmaneuvering the enemy for the purpose of rendering him powerless, in order to offer him the opportunity for restoration."[7] Or, you may choose to remain silent for the good of others, like the Nigerian military team who refused to reveal the whereabouts of the remaining Chibok girls who had been captured by the terrorist group Boko Haran. Using discernment, the team knew that silence was the wisest strategy; revealing the location of the girls could jeopardize their safety while the rescue plan was being carried out.[8]

Different Kinds of Eagles

When we communicate from a place of trust, we are free to choose the wisest, most life-giving method of expression for the situation and the relationship. However, our natural tendencies don't disappear entirely when we choose to be an Eagle. I have become more assertive as I've matured, but I will probably always be a little more passive than aggressive. And my friend Joy has softened a bit as she has grown, but she will probably always be a little more aggressive than passive. While neither of us are on the extreme ends of the assertiveness continuum any longer, we still are quite different in the way we communicate.

In this way, Eagles can take different forms, whether quiet, clever, or outspoken, reminiscent of the Turtle, the Fox, and the Bulldog. The distinction between these styles is that when they move up across the horizontal line on the diagram they are motivated not by fear but by trust. The Turtle, then, becomes a Thoughtful Eagle, the Fox becomes a Strategic Eagle, and the Bulldog becomes a Courageous Eagle. They don't have to move straight up, however. The Turtle may choose to be a Courageous Eagle in a particular situation, or the Bulldog may decide it's best to be more Thoughtful or Strategic. No matter the choice, the Eagle is marked by communication that stems from a place of trust for the purpose of truth and goodness and beauty.

Look again at the diagram again on the next page and then read the descriptions of the three types of Eagles.

Who is a *Thoughtful Eagle*? A Thoughtful Eagle is the faith-filled flip side of the Turtle. Excellent empathetic listeners, Thoughtful Eagles consider the feelings of others before speaking and are careful to phrase difficult information in a way that keeps the relational connection intact. No longer on the extreme end of "passive" like a Turtle, but still more quiet than outspoken, Thoughtful Eagles love well and listen well, yet are able to speak the truth with a balanced degree of assertiveness because of their faith in their ultimate acceptance by God. Thoughtful Eagles are valuable members of a team for their empathy.

Who is a *Strategic Eagle*? A Strategic Eagle is the faith-filled flip side of the Fox. Assertive and discerning, Strategic Eagles, or "Strateagles" (as my friend Jill calls them), intuitively read others well and are able to wisely phrase difficult information in a way that influences others towards good. No longer passive-aggressive, Strateagles discern when it's wisest to communicate indirectly and when it is wisest to communicate directly. Because they know Jesus has taken away their fear of shame, Strategic Eagles are able to be vulnerable, clearly expressing what they need, think, and feel. Strategic Eagles are valuable members of a team for their wisdom.

Who is a *Courageous Eagle*? A Courageous Eagle is the faith-filled flip side of the Bulldog. Boldly assertive, Courageous Eagles speak the truth with passion and conviction. While they are no longer on the extreme end of "aggressive," they are still more outspoken than quiet and are gifted at phrasing difficult information with truth and clarity. Trusting in God to do His work, Courageous Eagles are able to love, value, and affirm the voices and autonomy of others, and, by faith, believing that God is in control, they are able to offer freedom to those around them. Courageous Eagles are valuable members of a team for their boldness.

Each new, interactive moment presents a fresh opportunity to discern the wisest way to communicate. Instead of being locked into our fearful tendencies with a resigned, "That's just the way I am," we are free to speak in the next moment as a Thoughtful Eagle, a Strategic Eagle, or a Courageous Eagle, offering the most appropriate response for the situation, anchored by our trust in God.

LET'S TALK 6

1. *Are you most often a Thoughtful Eagle, a Strategic Eagle, or a Courageous Eagle?*

2. *Can you think of an example of when you communicated in this way? Describe it here.*

3. *How could others (at home, work, and in your community) benefit from your trust-based communication style?*

Empathetic

Discernment doesn't just help us know what and how to communicate. It also helps us to ask curious questions and then to listen well, using our Eagle vision to see an issue from the perspective of another person. And when we do, we are able to exercise another essential characteristic of the Eagle: empathy. The Thoughtful Eagle isn't the only one who is to be empathetic; all Eagles exercise empathy.

In the 1970's, "assertiveness training" was all the rage.[9] Women, especially, took classes to help them gain confidence in standing up for themselves. Yet, as my colleague, Peg, explained, the method was more like a "hit-and-run," shouting *at* someone and then bolting for the door rather than doing the more courageous thing of staying and engaging in a give-and-take conversation. And while it might have helped the women to feel strong, it eliminated the possibility for empathy.

Let's consider one misconception about empathy and then apply empathy to a difficult conversation in parenting.

Not weakness, strength

Some people think that the moment they express empathy they cease to have any power. Perhaps that's why empathy wasn't a part of assertiveness training. One woman in a communication training session I was leading at a community center, Rose, exemplified this perspective perfectly. She so feared seeming weak that she was incredulous at the idea of expressing her deeper emotions and empathizing with another person. She exclaimed, "Where do you live? Candyland? Because where I live if you do that they will eat you alive!" Instead of launching into a refutation of her accusation, I asked curious questions about her home and her relationships to try to better understand where she was coming from. And, once she described the abusive people in her life, I did understand. In fact, I empathized, saying, "That makes sense, Rose. If you think someone might hurt you, I can see how expressing empathy would feel really scary."

Empathy means slipping on a different pair of shoes to feel the emotions of the shoe-owner. I do this by listening for key words and watching body language. While Rose never said the word "scared," the idea of being eaten alive would make any of us feel afraid, so I knew *fear* was the emotion she was feeling. Her agitated body language also suggested fear. And then she affirmed I was right, nodding, "H---, yeah." Knowing her fear, I was able to then gently lead her and another woman into a role-play conversation where they could experience communicating from empathy in a safe environment. It was a deeply emotional and unforgettable experience for all of us in the room.

There have been times in my life I have been afraid I would be hurt if I showed any sign of weakness, so it wasn't difficult to empathize with Rose. But if someone describes a situation that seems foreign to you, it might be a bit more of a stretch. So, ask yourself, "What if?" as in "What if I were in that situation? How would I feel?" If you can land on an emotion, such as "hurt," then think back to other situations in which you have felt hurt. Remembering the sensation of that emotion can help you empathize. Then, you're able to say honestly, "I can understand how you would feel hurt. I have felt that way before."

Clearly, empathy requires that we are aware of our own pain. In fact, I asked a professor at Vanderbilt University what texts she utilizes to teach empathy to the medical professionals in her classes. She said she doesn't use a text but instead teaches the students how to live mindfully, recognizing and feeling their own pain and fear in the present and from the past. It is only when we are aware of our own pain and fear that we can be empathetic with others, feeling their pain and fear with them.

Finding empathy for another person's pain is the key to communicating in compassionate ways while still drawing necessary boundaries to protect yourself. And, to be clear, seeing a situation from another perspective doesn't mean you ever need to justify someone's unkind words or actions. Your empathy, instead, is fueled by your Eagle vision that is able to perceive the fear motivating an unhealthy communicator. Often, fear is hidden behind anger. And it takes a strong, mature Eagle to respond to anger with empathy, especially when the anger is directed at you. But remember the diagram? It's fear that's underneath the Turtle's reticence, the Fox's manipulation, and the Bulldog's aggression. And it's trust in *Whose* we are that allows us to empathize and respond with compassion to the unhealthy communicator. Instead of empathy signifying weakness, it actually signifies strength.

Parenting

Parenting is a rather challenging case in communicating empathy. A few nights ago, I found one of my sons playing a video game in his room instead of doing his homework. I told him it was time for bed.

"But mom, I need to stay up and finish my homework!" he pleaded.

"Oh man, do you have a lot left?

"Yeah! I still have two pages of math problems." He takes out the sheets and shows me.

"Wow. That looks tough. Unfortunately, it's bedtime right now, though."

"I can't get a zero on these pages, Mom! I have to stay up and do them."

"I know. I never wanted to get zeros on my homework either. But since you have to go to bed now, what are you doing to do?"

He puts his forehead down on his desk with a "thwunk."

"Ouch. Don't hurt yourself. Let's see," I offer, "You could get up early tomorrow morning and do them before school?"

""But I'm going to be soooo tired if I have to get up early!"

"I know. I'm sad for you. It stinks to be tired all day. Do you need me to help you set your alarm?"

My job as a parent is to set the boundary by enforcing the consequence (going to bed), yet still express empathy for my son's situation (having to get up early or not finishing his homework). *Parenting with Love and Logic* teaches that the more I'm able to empathize and respond in compassionate ways to his situation the more my son will see that his choices are the problem, not his mother.[10]

Empathy and assertiveness necessarily co-exist in the Eagle communicator; we can speak the truth *and* express compassion in a way that values the heart of the other person at the same time. The truth is, every one of us has priceless value; we all are made in the image of God.

LET'S TALK 7
When is it easy for you to express empathy and when is it difficult? Why do you think this is the case?

Forward-thinking

In the midst of a tough conversation, it's quite challenging to remember that the other person was made in the image of God and to express empathy and value. Yet, these are necessary components to keeping a relational connection alive. Embroiled in head-to-head combat to get our needs met, we often find ourselves saying what will help us get what we want the most quickly. But Eagle communicators know that short-run needs don't justify short-tempered words and that the long-run consequences of short-tempered words have a high price tag. That's why Eagles are forward-thinking.

Let's consider the impact of forward-thinking communication on just two areas of our lives- our communities and our families.

Our communities

Take, for instance, Brianne. When painters left her house after painting her railing and doing a shoddy job, she knew she needed to call and confront them. She could have chosen to use insulting words but instead she chose to ask curious questions, respond with empathy, and then express her needs firmly and confidently, valuing the hearts of the painters. Her communication showed that she was living out the guideline from Matthew 7:12, "...treat people the same way you want them to treat you..." The painters apologized, came back, and repainted her railing to her satisfaction. Weeks later, on a Sunday morning, she turned to greet the man behind her, only to find it was one of the painters! Had she insulted him or spoken unkindly it would have been an uncomfortable greeting, for sure. But because she had made Eagle choices in her tough conversation, their relational connection was still intact.

Our communities are entwined enough that it just isn't worth it to burn bridges. Like when Ryan switched jobs only to find that his new boss used to be one of the employees under him at a previous company. Or when Allison found that the grouchy receptionist at her dentist office was the parent of a boy on her son's soccer team. We never know when we will need to interact in a new context with someone from our past. Communicating from a place of trust with discernment and empathy allows us to keep connections alive in our communities.

Our families

Nowhere is the impact of communication more felt than in our families. Those who know us best often get the brunt of our fear-based, default communication styles. We blurt what we're thinking, hide what we're feeling, and snap without warning, all to get the people in our family to do what we want them to do so we can get our needs met. But if we stop for a moment and slow everything down, remembering the health and connection we want in the long run, we can choose our words in a way that honestly expresses what we're feeling and what we need and at the same time values the hearts of the people in our family.

A while ago, I was doing dishes in the kitchen after dinner while my husband was reading a book on our most comfortable brown chair in the living room. I was annoyed, and thought, "Why does he get to sit out there reading a book while I'm in here slaving away in the kitchen?" A lot like Shari at the beginning of Session Six, I slammed a few drawers and cupboards in hopes that he would notice my frustration and ask what was wrong. He finally did. "Honey, is everything okay out there?" I was silent for a few minutes while I scrubbed a pan. He asked again, "Honey?"

I suddenly became a snapping turtle. I stopped scrubbing and glared into the living room, wishing I could make darts shoot out of my eyes. Instead, I shot darts out of my mouth. "You know what? You don't do jack! You mow. That's it. And I do everything else. And you just...mow." I knew that wasn't true, but sometimes it feels really good to exaggerate.

He put his book down on the arm of the chair, got up, and walked into the kitchen. He crossed to the side of the kitchen counter nearest me. "Wow, babe. Is that really how you feel?" Suddenly, I was ashamed at the blatant immaturity of my outburst and started scrubbing the pan really hard. I hated doing dishes by myself. It made me feel so...lonely.

The thought was an epiphany. I stopped scrubbing and looked at Brian. "Actually, I feel...I feel really lonely when I'm out here by myself. I would love it if we could do the dishes together."

"Sure," he said, and picked up a towel to dry a dripping colander from the dish drainer.

Later that night I admitted sheepishly, "I know you do more than mow. Sorry I said you don't do jack." He graciously forgave me.

The next morning I came downstairs to find a note on the kitchen counter. It read, "Went out for a run. Back at 7:15. Love, Jack." And Jack has written me love notes ever since.

Brian "spoke Eagle" when he chose to engage my accusation with curious questions instead of defensive or attacking statements. He was forward-thinking, keeping his connection with me alive, even in the midst of our conflict. For me, when I had the courage to be vulnerable, expressing my deeper, softer emotion of "lonely," I also became an Eagle. Since then, we have continued to keep the conversation open, revisiting the division of household chores often to keep resentment from building up.

Being a forward-thinking communicator is worth it, not only for healthy relationships now, but for healthy relationships 30 years from now in our communities and our families.

LET'S TALK 8

Describe a situation in which you were not forward-thinking in your communication and suffered the consequences, or when you were forward-thinking and reaped the benefits.

As we mature as leaders in our trust, discernment, empathy, and forward-thinking mindset, we can't stay Turtles, Foxes, and Bulldogs. Learning to trust more fully in the Lord and to communicate from a place of positive strength, we grow into Thoughtful Eagles, Strategic Eagles, and Courageous Eagles, all valuable styles of leadership. Yes, we'll have moments where we default back into our fear-based styles, but with the guidance of our Helper, the Holy Spirit, we will experience many more moments where we speak Eagle and soar.

WORDS FROM THE WORD

You knew this was coming. If the Turtle, the Fox, and the Bulldog all had biblical characters to represent them, the Eagle needs one as well. And since there was only one perfect communicator, the biblical character for the Eagle is...you guessed it...Jesus! Jesus was the ultimate Trusting, Discerning, Empathetic, Forward-thinking communicator.

1. *Who and what did Jesus trust? (John 5:17, 6:38, 8:29)*

2. *Jesus was always discerning, choosing the appropriate response for a given situation.*

    a. *When was He a Thoughtful Eagle? (Is. 53:7, Matt. 26:63)*

    b. *A Strategic Eagle? (Luke 20:1-8)*

c. A Courageous Eagle? (Luke 19:45-46)

3. *How do you know Jesus was empathetic? Look for a verse about it and write it here:*

4. *How was Jesus forward-thinking? (John 7:8, Hebrews 12:2)*

As we read the Word knowing that Jesus is the best example of an Eagle communicator, it is important to remember that He was God and we are not. As God, it was His prerogative to call the pious Pharisees "whitewashed tombs." For us, on the other hand, we must exercise extreme caution when calling out the character of others. The Word makes it very clear in James 4:12 that judging is God's job, not ours: "There is only one Lawgiver and Judge, the One who is able to save and to destroy; but who are you who judge your neighbor?"

As God's Son, Jesus had divine vision, able to see into the thoughts and intentions of each heart and also able to see the cross set before Him. He truly partnered with the Father and never strayed from doing His will. Even when His sweat was like "great drops of blood" in the garden as He asked if the Father would take the cup of suffering from Him, He spoke with faith, saying, "...yet not my will, but Yours be done" (Luke 22:42). Jesus was able to be an Eagle communicator because of His connection to the Father. And even on the cross when he felt the agony of disconnection, pleading, "MY GOD, MY GOD, WHY HAVE YOU FORSAKEN ME?" (Matthew 27:46), we know even then He chose to trust His Father's will as He breathed His last, "Father, INTO YOUR HANDS I COMMIT MY SPIRIT" (Luke 23:46).

Jesus truly soared with the power of the Holy Spirit in His communication, standing firm against temptation (Matthew 4), speaking hope, and even offering forgiveness to His accusers (Luke 23:34). Whether He was thoughtful, strategic, or courageous, we know every word He said was motivated not by fear of people but by trust in His Father. May we follow His example, soaring on faith through our toughest conversations as we wait patiently on the Father to do His work.

CREATIVE EXERCISE- "Soaring Eagle" (complete on your own and then share during group time)
In the space on the next page, draw a soaring eagle with wings outstretched. Write your first name on one wing and your last (or middle) name on the second wing. Write out Isaiah 40:31 somewhere on the page. Now write adjectives in the space around the eagle that describe how you would like to

communicate with those in your family, your neighborhood, your community, your workplace, and your world.

Final Thoughts on Connection

Throughout this study, we have discussed how connection is one of our greatest needs and disconnection is one of our greatest fears. Kenneth Burke, a rhetorical theorist, explains that our desire to connect with each other is rooted in our initial separation from our mothers when the umbilical cord was cut. And yes, that was a dramatic separation. Burke believed all of our communicative attempts to persuade others (through both talking and silence) are aimed at restoring that lost connection, not just with our mothers but with everyone around us. When we do experience a connection with others by finding a way to identify with them Burke believed we then share "substance," such as the substance of our desire for connection. Since you and I both share this desire or "substance," we then are what Burke calls, "consubstantial."[11]

But let's look at Burke's theory of consubstantiality through a different lens. What if our desire for connection is rooted in a separation that goes back even further than our mothers? What if it is an echo of an "ancient longing for reunion with one from whom we have long been separated?"[12]

We, God's beloved, who walked and talked with our Creator as friends in the cool of the evening, experiencing communion and community and consubstantiality, were suddenly severed by our sin. We disobeyed God's command to not eat of the Tree of Good and Evil and we sunk our teeth deep into the fruit of defiance. Our connection, built from truth and beauty and love, was severed, inviting miscommunication, mistrust, suspicion, lying, and hiding. We were sent from the Garden, hopelessly separated from God.

We tried to make things right, to repent with apologies and sacrifices. Yet, the canyon of our sin was too wide for us to bridge with our meager apologies. Nothing we could sacrifice would be worthy enough or perfect enough to restore our connection.

Until Jesus.

When God sent Jesus, His Son, His lifeblood, to live on earth and then to be sacrificed for us on the cross, He offered us the "substance" of Himself, His body, His blood. And as we accept His sacrifice as our salvation, God's plan all along to reconnect us with Himself, we are brought back into communion with Him where we can walk and talk in the cool of the evening as friends.

Jesus modeled how we were to remember and re-experience our connection: communion. As we eat the bread and drink the cup of communion, we identify with His sacrifice, we chew, we ruminate, we let the drink flow deep, sending nourishment and hope into the dark, lonely places in our souls. As we share His substance, we taste "consubstantiality" with our Creator.

Yet, our connection with God here on earth is still is only a shadow of what it will be one day. That's why C.S. Lewis called our earth the "shadowlands,"[13] because we now only "see in a mirror dimly, but then face to face" (I Cor. 13:12).

TALK TO GOD

As you close your time together, spend some time in prayer, thanking God for giving us the example of Jesus. Then, humbly ask God for:

courage to commit to partnering with Him for life

keen vision to be aware of yourself and observant of the needs of others

discernment to know when to be quiet, when to be strategic, and when to be outspoken

the empathy necessary to respond with compassion

and the Holy Spirit to fill you so that you can soar on His power.

SESSION EIGHT
SOAR

Maureen breathed deeply for a moment as she put her hand on the door of the southern coffee shop. Even though she had *assessed her safety* and chosen a neutral location, she knew this conversation wouldn't be easy. Glancing in the window, she could see Alice, her blonde hair pulled back into a ponytail, sitting at a table already and looking at her phone. Maureen pushed the door open and approached the table.

"Hi!" she said, smiling.

"Oh, hi!" Alice replied, setting her phone down. Maureen took her place across from Alice, nestled her small handbag next to her on the bench, took off her teal scarf and pulled her brown hair out of the collar of her jacket. "Brrr! It's chilly out there this morning!"

"Yeah, tell me about it," Alice said, rolling her blue eyes. "When I lived in California we never had to deal with weather like this."

"Oh, I'm sure you..."

Alice cut her off. "I mean, it was always sunny and warm and except for the Santa Ana winds that surprised us some days it was perfect. You know I used to surf, right? Well, those winds were actually what made the waves amazing so we used to pray for them to..."

Alice continued, talking about her life in Southern California- how she had thought about being a meteorologist and once fell in love with a red-haired surfer named Harley. Maureen had actually heard most of these stories before, as Alice referred to them often during their small group Bible study. And Alice was always quick to piggy-back one of her stories onto someone else's story.

As the leader of the small group, Maureen was fully aware of how the other group members had little time to share because Alice monopolized the discussion. Julie and Rhonda, two other group members, had both mentioned to Maureen on separate occasions how they wished Alice wouldn't talk so much- which was when Maureen decided it was time to initiate a difficult conversation with Alice.

Maureen knew it was a tricky situation. Alice was in the midst of a painful divorce and needed their support. With her self-esteem shot by an abusive husband, she was in a fragile state already. Maureen had been praying that the Holy Spirit would fill her with wisdom and discernment to know how to approach Alice with humility, speak the truth in love, find a way to keep Alice's self-esteem intact, and keep the heart connection between them alive. But she was nervous.

A bubbly server approached and provided a natural break in Alice's monologue. Alice ordered a coffee and Maureen asked for a cranberry juice. When the server left, the thought crossed Maureen's mind that she could launch into the difficult part of the conversation now. And yet, it felt too early. Broaching the risky topic too soon could make for a rather long and awkward breakfast, or a very short breakfast if Alice got offended and left. And Alice might be hungry, which would not help her emotional coping skills at grappling

178

with difficult information. Maureen decided it would be best to ask a few questions first to hear Alice's heart and discern her current state regarding her disintegrating marriage.

"So, what do you hear from Craig these days?"

"Nothing," Alice said. "He's being really quiet. A little too quiet, I think. I guess he's hired some hotshot lawyer now."

"Really? Wow. How do you feel about that?" Maureen asked.

"It worries me. I really don't know what he wants. And I don't have the money to hire a lawyer like that. But if he's trying to fight me to get custody of the kids, that's not going to happen."

Maureen could read every emotion that crossed Alice's face. Anxiety, fear, anger. A concern for finances. She could at least assuage that part of the equation this morning.

"I don't blame you. That would scare me, too. And just so you know, breakfast is on me, so order whatever you'd like."

"Maureen! You don't have to do that."

"I want to," Maureen replied. "You have enough to worry about."

"Thanks."

The bubbly server was back with their drinks, took their omelet orders, and left. Maureen debated again about jumping into the deep end, but again decided to wait- at least until the food arrived. She didn't want the server interrupting their conversation when she brought the omelets. Instead, Maureen asked a few more questions about Alice's life- her kids and her work as an insurance agent.

Soon, the server was carrying out sizzling omelets and set them on the table. "Anything else I can get for you?"

"I think we're good. Thanks!" Maureen looked at Alice. "I'll pray for us." After a short prayer, she took a deep breath. It was time.

"Alice, I..." Maureen started. But at the same time, Alice remarked, "Ooh. This looks yummy."

As Alice took a bite, Maureen tried again. "I'm really glad you could meet with..."

But again, Alice interrupted, this time with her mouth full. "The grt thng abt omlts is tht you cn hide all srts of vggies in 'em. I once mde an omlt with sqush n zucchni n..."

Maureen knew her first task was to bring up the topic of their small group. How could she connect omelets and small group? She quickly broke into Alice's monologue, bringing up another small group member.

"Oh that's right. Laura told me she and her roommate have an amazing garden full of veggies in their backyard. I think she's one of those people who have all sorts of hidden talents. I love it that our group is so diverse, don't you?"

"Yeah, let's see," Alice replied, thinking. "We have an architect, a teacher, an artist..."

"So, how are you feeling about our group? Are you liking the study so far?" Maureen asked, and took a bite of her omelet. Finally, they were getting closer to the topic.

"Sure, I like it." Alice used her fork to pick out a mushroom and ate it. "I mean, it's tough to find the time to do the homework, but when I do, I get a lot out of it. And even if I don't do it, I think our discussions are really good."

Now came the tricky part. "Yeah, I love our discussions, too." Maureen said. She knew she needed to *start by telling Alice something she valued about her.* "One of the things I appreciate about you is how you share so vulnerably. You're really open about the things that are going on in your life."

"You don't think it's too much?" Alice asked.

Alice had volleyed the ball directly into Maureen's hand. But Maureen waited. She wanted to communicate a little more value first before the spike. "I think being open is a really good quality. I'm hoping your openness will encourage some of the other women to be open, too."

"Thanks. Sometimes I wonder if I share too much."

Clearly, Alice was already afraid that she talked too much, which clued Maureen in that Alice was insecure about it and possibly feared that she would be rejected for her wealth of words. Because of this, along with her distinct awareness of their Southern culture, Maureen felt that a more indirect strategy would be the most beneficial in this situation. At the same time, it was essential that she truthfully *offer her own story*. She decided to come at the problem from a creative angle.

"You know, one of the things I've noticed is that some of the women hesitate to share. I'm kind of an introvert, so I know how they feel. It's like you almost have to ask me point-blank what I'm thinking if I'm going to share anything," Maureen chuckled. She looked at Alice, "Have you noticed that some of the women are kind of hesitant, too?"

"Yeah, they are." Alice shook her head. "I can't relate to that at all," she laughed.

Maureen then asked a curious question. "So what are you thinking when they're all being quiet?"

Alice laughed again. "I'm thinking, 'Somebody needs to talk, here!' I can't stand it when everybody's quiet. So I guess that's why I jump in and say stuff."

Maureen knew how awkward silence could feel in a small group, so she was able to *respond with empathy*. "I know. It feels awkward when it's quiet, doesn't it?"

"So awkward! And then I start thinking, 'I need to fix this- and fast!'"

"I know. Me too. But I've been wondering how we could encourage the other women to share."

Maureen was really proud of herself for being so clever. But Alice paused for a moment, picked at her omelet, then stared across the table. "Oh, I get it. You're doing this because everybody thinks I talk too much, aren't you, Maureen?"

Maureen could feel her heart start to race. Her mouth went instantly dry and her omelet went out of focus. Then, she felt nauseous, almost like Alice had punched her in the stomach. It took every ounce of self-control to stay in her seat and to not excuse herself to go the bathroom and disappear. The shame she felt for having offended her friend was almost suffocating.

But she stayed. She released the shame, reminding herself that this conversation was necessary for the good of the whole group- and for Alice's good as well. She took a deep breath, looked back at Alice. Then, she acknowledged her body's response. "Just so you know, I'm suddenly feeling my heart racing. This is really hard for me, Alice, because you're my friend and I care about you." And then she asked another curious question to help Alice assess her own state. "What are you feeling right now?"

Alice's eyes filled with tears as she looked away then back at her coffee cup. "Like I'm stupid. Like I should just quit the group." One tear fell and she quickly wiped it away.

"You aren't stupid," Maureen said quietly. She knew Alice was probably feeling debilitating shame and disconnection, so she reached across the table and put her hand on Alice's. "You have a lot going on in your life right now and I do want you to be able to share it."

182

Alice pulled her hand away. "Well, I won't. I won't share anything. I'll just keep my big mouth shut."

Now it was time to be firmly loving. "Alice, look at me."

Alice turned her blue eyes to look at Maureen's. "We're all on the same team. And for our group to work, we need *everyone* to share equally. That includes you. And I was hoping we could work together to come up with a solution."

"What, for the problem of me talking so much?"

"For the hope that everyone would have equal time to share and feel as open as you do to tell us what's going on in their lives. I'm sure you want that, too."

"Of course I do."

Now that they had a common goal in mind, Maureen suggested a solution. "I did have one idea," Maureen offered. "What if we think of some curious questions we could ask the other women in the group?"

"Like what? Like, 'Why are you all so quiet?'" Alice rolled her eyes.

"Yeah, I'm sure that would make them want to open right up!" Maureen chuckled. Alice hinted a smile. Maureen suddenly noticed her heart had stopped racing and her breathing had become more natural. She took a sip of her cranberry juice.

"I'm kidding," Alice smiled.

"I know. So, maybe we could ask questions that don't start with the word 'why.' Have you ever noticed how 'why' questions seem to make people defensive?"

"Why do you wanna know?" Alice smiled again. Then she asked, "So what kinds of questions don't make people defensive?"

"Like *that* question!" Maureen exclaimed. "It started with the word 'What' and asks me to process something. So maybe we could ask something like, 'What are you thinking about this, Rhonda?'"

Alice chimed in. "Or 'How can you relate to this, Julie?'

Maureen smiled. "Exactly."

Alice grinned slyly. "Or maybe 'What's the worst sin you've ever committed, Laura?'" Then she laughed, "Hey, it started with 'What'!"

Maureen laughed, too. "Okay, so there might be a few 'what' questions that could make people feel defensive."

"Yeah, don't make *me* answer that one," Alice said, using her fork to stack a few bell peppers.

"I won't," Maureen smiled, "At least not right now."

The two of them laughed again, and Maureen realized, by God's grace, that Alice had been able to receive the difficult information and that their connection was still intact. She knew, however, over the coming weeks, that there would be times Alice would start to feel that familiar shame and might again feel the urge to quit the group. It would be essential that Maureen create a path that would keep the conversation open and help them *move forward together*.

"Hey, so maybe after our next group you and I could get together again and talk about how you think it went? It might take a little practice for us to get used to coming up with curious questions."

"Okay, sure," Alice responded, "and that would give me more time with you, too. Maybe we could have lunch every week right after the study?"

"Yeah, maybe. Although I'm not sure I could do it every week..."

She would have to leave it at that for now. A boundary-setting conversation would take more energy and courage, and she was fresh out of both of those for today. For Alice, she now had the freedom to learn the new skill of asking curious questions within the safe environment of a small group who accepted her. Or, she could ignore the plan and keep monopolizing the discussion, or she could quit the group.

No matter what Alice decided to do, Maureen knew that was up to Alice. For Maureen, she had done what God had asked her to do- communicate from a place of trust, trusting that God values the voice of every person in her group and that He had placed her in a position of leadership. Knowing Alice's fragility, she was able to approach the topic in an indirect way so that Alice would be more likely to receive it. She also trusted that Alice was monopolizing the discussion not because she was insensitive, but because she was insecure and afraid. This gave her the ability to exercise compassion and empathy for her group member. And Maureen was able to be forward-thinking, speaking words of affirmation and value that kept her connection with Alice alive.

LET'S TALK 1
1. *In what way did Maureen's faith give her the courage and freedom to speak Eagle in this conversation?*

2. *How might a Bulldog, a Fox, or a Turtle approach (or not approach) someone like Alice?*

Bulldog:

Fox:

Turtle:

3. *What if Alice had stormed out of the restaurant and quit the group? How could Maureen have responded from a place of faith?*

When we take a closer look at the each of the steps that Maureen followed in her interaction with Alice, it's an acrostic that spells the word, S.O.A.R. Let's explore each of these steps individually.

SOAR: 4 Steps to Connection in Tough Conversations

Before you SOAR:
Assess the Situation

Start with Value
Offer your Story
Ask Curious Questions
Respond with Empathy

To keep SOARing:
Move Forward Together

BEFORE YOU SOAR:

Before you SOAR through a tough conversation, *Assess the Situation.* Consider your safety and bring someone with you if you think your safety is in jeopardy. Choose a neutral location, like a coffee shop or a park, and the day and time that you think will be best for yourself and the other person. Spend time in prayer, asking God to give you the wisdom to communicate like an Eagle in this conversation.

Now...SOAR!

S- Start with Value

Broach the topic by first speaking value. Valuing another person speaks life, affirming what is specifically good and true and beautiful in the other person. Consider who the person is, what he or she does or gives, strengths, abilities, or passions, and your history, memories, or relationship. Think about his or her contribution to your life, or to the world, and find something to communicate that you value. If you have a hard time thinking of something you value personally, ask yourself, "What does God value about this person?" For the greatest connection, position yourself physically on the person's level, making eye contact while you express value.

LET'S TALK 2

With an upcoming difficult conversation in mind, what is something you could communicate that you value about the other person?

O- Offer Your Story

Explain the "story" behind what brought you to initiate this conversation or how you came to this conclusion, position, or decision. Understand that the word "story" here is rather broad. Sometimes our stories may only consist of our perspective on a situation, or they may include how we came across research or data, when we first read a particular book or heard a speech, watched a movie or a play, and heard a sermon or met a person that has impacted our thoughts and feelings on this issue.

Or, if you're discussing a current conflict in your relationship, try phrasing your journey in terms of a beginning, middle, and end (or future) of your story. Such as describing your initial dreams and hopes for this situation or relationship, then how you first began to notice something amiss, and how today you long to realize the dream for your good and the good of the other person.

Or, maybe consider it in terms of the redemption cycle from Caesar Kalinowski's Gospel Primer- Creation (when things were good), Fall (when things turned bad), Redemption (what could turn it around) and Restoration (a view of the beautiful future).[1] As much as possible, communicate the future not in terms of what you are afraid of, but in positive terms, such as what you hope for or long to experience and what you desire for the other person to experience.

The power of story, your story, cannot be emphasized enough. Neuroscience research has shown that when someone tells a story, our brains release positive neurotransmitters like oxytocin and dopamine that help us connect with the storyteller, as if we are "inside" the story.[2] As Thompson writes, "...the power of storytelling goes beyond the border of the story itself. It moves into the nooks and crannies of our memories and emotions, sometimes gently, sometimes explosively, revealing, awakening, shocking, calling."[3]

Say it brave. Tell your story.

LET'S TALK 3
What's your story? In the difficult conversation you noted in Let's Talk 2, write out what you could share with the other person about your journey and perspective regarding the risky topic.

Ask Curious Questions

Formulate curious questions in which you truly seek to understand the perspective of the other person. Phrase your questions beginning with the word "What," "How," or the phrase "Tell me more about..." instead of the word "Why." The word "Why" often is the beginning of a loaded question- a question that is really a statement. "Why do you act that way?" really means, "You shouldn't act that way." Being asked "Why" triggers the amygdala. Remember the amygdala? It's the primitive part of our brain that tells us to defend ourselves because we are in danger. So, we might fight, freeze, or flee,[4] none of which are helpful for a conversation. "Why" begins a personal question whose answer is embedded inside us. Consider the questions, "Why do you...?" or "Why are you...?" These are identity questions and act as triggers, summoning our weapons to defend and protect our soft interior and shut down the threatening conversation.

On the other hand, a "what" question implies that the problem is "this thing out here in front of us that we can look at together." A "what" question has an answer that, instead of being embedded inside us and tied to our self-image, can be exterior, even between us, where we can see it and talk about it. To answer, we must use our prefrontal cortex, the part of our brain that can reason and process information and emotions.

However, not all "What" questions are curious. For instance, stay away from the "what" question, "What were you thinking?" which is really the statement, "That was stupid," and would undoubtedly conjure the boxing gloves. Instead, try phrasing your query with true curiosity, such as, "Tell me more about..." or "Help me understand what was..."

LET'S TALK 4
What are some curious questions you could ask the other person in this interaction?

Respond with Empathy

When the other party responds to your curious questions, listen actively, putting yourself in his or her shoes to empathize. Often, we may not be able to empathize with the exact content of a particular situation, but we can empathize with the universal emotions that the person might have experienced, such as hurt, anger, loneliness, confusion, fear, shame, sadness, etc. So, we can say empathetically, "I know how it feels to be afraid. I can see how you would feel that way." Responding with empathy can help others to feel heard, understood, and valued.

LET'S TALK 5

Consider the emotions the other person might have experienced in the past or might experience during your conversation. Believe the best about the emotions of the other person. What can you say to empathize with those emotions?

Since a conversation is dynamic, less like a line between a sender and a receiver and more like an interactive circle, these aren't a set of steps you can follow in order and then shut the door. During the conversation, you may need to reiterate value and you'll probably need to revisit your story, perhaps phrasing it in a different way to help the other party understand. There will also be other curious questions that will come to mind to ask throughout your interaction, and it's wise to offer empathy all along the way.

To Keep Soaring...

At some point, however, you'll need to bring the conversation to a close. To move forward, help the other person visualize how you are on the same team, working together towards a solution or a common goal. Invite ideas for solutions. Collaborate on the best way for you to both get your needs met in this situation or relationship. Sometimes, continuing to soar may mean that you don't land on a viable solution and perhaps don't even try to fix it, but you agree to hold the tension of disagreement.

For the Eagle, brave conversations don't really end. The door to dialogue must be left open for whenever either of you would like to revisit the same topic again in the future. Emotions are deep and lasting and healthy processing takes place not just in one conversation but over a long period of time.

WORDS FROM THE WORD

Read Isaiah 6:1-8.

1. *The seraphim above the throne of the Lord were calling to each other, "Holy, holy, holy is the* LORD *Almighty; the whole earth is full of his glory" (NIV).[5] Our English word "holy," is "hagios" in the Greek.[6] Look up what the word "hagios" means online and write it here:*

_____

2. How might this definition of "holy" inform the way we are to communicate?

3. In what way have you been a man or woman of "unclean lips," living among a people of "unclean lips?"

4. From where did the seraphim take the coal? Why might this have been significant?

5. What did touching Isaiah's lips with the live coal represent?

6. *How might the action with the hot coal have prepared Isaiah for how he responded to the Lord's question?*

If you have put your faith in Jesus Christ for your salvation, your sin is forgiven and you no longer have to be ashamed of your unworthiness or afraid of punishment. Jesus is worthy and your shame was crucified with Him for good. For good! You are forgiven, loved, and free, and you can now speak forgiveness, love, and freedom to others.

The journey from fear to trust in the way we communicate is not easy. But the rewards are worth it. A few years ago, I was in a book club. One evening, a woman in the group was trying to be funny and said something that deeply hurt me. I called her afterwards, and, shaking in my shoes, I told her that because I valued my relationship with her I needed to let her know that I was hurting. She assured me she hadn't meant to hurt me. It was a brief conversation.

A few days later, she asked if she could come by my house. I agreed. We sat on my back deck over lemonade to talk about the incident. She offered a tearful, heartfelt apology; I extended authentic forgiveness. I asked curious questions about what might have motivated her comment and expressed empathy for the emotions she had been feeling in that moment. She asked curious questions and expressed empathy for me. We moved forward together in our friendship, building on what we had experienced in that conversation.

Later, I received the following email from her:

"Thank you for telling me how my comment made you feel. You made the courageous decision to trust Him, push into it with me at His prompting. That moment has forever changed my way of thinking, relating, and speaking. Up to that moment, I had almost no filter and no self-control. That excruciating event led to my eyes being opened and a night of wrestling with God as He set me free from deeply ingrained, unhealthy (sinful) relational patterns. It is a crossroads in my life.

Through the terror and pain of exposure, I was healed of an ancient wound and set free. Who knew what would happen if we actually decide to take Him at His word and speak the truth in love?"

As I read her email, I wept. God is at work. Always.

CREATIVE EXERCISE- "Anointed Communication"
During your small group time, your leader will guide you and your fellow group members through Isaiah 6:1-8 to help you experience it in a new way.

TALK TO GOD
In this final time of prayer...

> *repent for the ways you have not communicated from a place of trust in the past*

> *thank God specifically for what He has taught you during this study*

> *thank God for your fellow group members*

> *pray for specific requests regarding upcoming interactions*

> *pray that the Lord would help you have the faith and courage to SOAR*

> *and finally, believe God for what He can do in you and through you in the future!*

SAY IT BRAVE
Suggestions for Leaders

In preparing to lead your small group, read the following suggestions prior to each session.

SESSION ONE: Introduction (120 minutes)

Your first group meeting does not require any reading or preparation from your group members as they will be receiving this study, *Say It Brave*, for the first time. Once you give them their books at the beginning of the meeting, the elements listed below are also included for them to follow along in Session One at the beginning of this study. The following suggestions give you further ideas in how to lead this session and how much time you may want to allow for each section before moving on to the next.

1. **Welcome** (5 minutes): Welcome your group members, hand out their books, and explain why you chose this material.

2. **Introductions** (15 minutes): Invite your group members to introduce themselves with their name, something about their family, vocation, and/or where they live, and what they hope to gain from this study.

3. **Letter from the Author** (5 minutes): Take turns reading the paragraphs of the letter aloud- or have one person read the letter in its entirety.

4. **Prayer** (2 minutes): Pray that God would open the eyes of your hearts while you read His word.

5. **Words from the Word** (25 minutes): Ask your group members to take out their Bibles or Bible apps and take turns reading out loud through all of Proverbs 15. It is fine for them to use different versions as this provides the opportunity to mention the differences.

   In counting the number of verses on the elements of communication, keep in mind that there isn't one right answer; group members will probably come up with different numbers depending on the version they were reading. Discuss their answers and encourage them to think of other verses or stories from scripture to support their thoughts.

6. **Let's Talk** (33 minutes): The discussion questions address participants' fear of tough conversations. Invite them to share their own level of fear and be sure to share your own.

7. **Creative Exercise- "Snapshots"** (20 minutes): In this exercise, invite the participants to think of a posture that represents their personal attitude toward tough conversations. If they need help thinking of something, tell them they can ask you or the other group members for help. For instance, if Julie is afraid of offending someone, she might simply put her hands over her mouth. If Ron likes difficult conversations because he has strong opinions and doesn't mind expressing them, he might stand up and cup his hands around his mouth like a megaphone. Invite each participant to demonstrate his or her posture for the group. Encourage your group members that there isn't a "right" posture. Whatever he or

she does is fine. Even if a group member isn't sure of his or her attitude, you can assist in coming up with an "I don't know" posture. Be sure to show them your posture, as well.

Once your group members have demonstrated their postures, group them according to their attitudes, with similar attitudes standing together to create one frozen picture for the rest of the participants to observe. Invite the participants to comment on each other's postures and ask curious questions about them.

You can also line them up according to their postures with the most fearful posture on one end and the least fearful posture on the other end. This will be a very subjective order, so don't worry about "getting it right." Allow each group member to step out for a moment to see the others in the line.

Now, instruct two participants to stand with their frozen postures and face each other to create a still picture of two people having a difficult conversation. Ask your group members engaging questions, such as, "What do you think this dialogue would be like?," "How would you feel if you were that person?," and "What would make this interaction challenging?" Invite the participants, again, to make comments and ask curious questions. Other duos may follow suit if time permits.

Finally, invite participants to create a snapshot that represents the attitude they hope to have toward tough conversations by the end of this study. Share your own posture, as well.

8. **Talk to God** (15 minutes): You have countless options for how to lead your prayer time this week and the weeks to follow. You can pair up participants to pray for each other, invite everyone to pray silently, ask anyone who feels comfortable to pray out loud, invite them to pray for the person on their right, or take requests and then you close in prayer...the list goes on! You can even try all praying at once like believers in Japanese churches! In any case, if you would like your group members to pray out loud, be sure to ask them if they are comfortable with it before bowing your heads. If someone is not comfortable with it, give that person the freedom to pray silently.

While I've offered a brief list of things to pray for this week, feel free to revise them or add your own.

For next week: Remind participants to read Session Two, to write down their thoughts in the spaces provided, and come prepared to discuss the concepts.

SESSION TWO: Tough Conversations- A Dreaded Necessity (120 minutes)

1. **Welcome, check-in, and opening prayer** (10 minutes): Welcome your group members. Invite one volunteer to share about a difficult conversation from this past week. Try to keep this very brief. Remember to not "fix," but instead to ask curious questions to further understand this person's thoughts and feelings. Before you open your books to discuss the content of this session, pray for your time together.

2. **Discussion** (20 minutes): Invite your group members to share what they wrote down in answer to the questions in Let's Talk 1-2.

3. **Words from the Word** (30 minutes): Ask for a volunteer to read Mark 4:35-41 aloud.

   Then, read aloud the section in this book beginning with "Jesus had a lot to say about fear…" and ending with "In need. In dependence. In faith."

   Invite participants to discuss their responses to the questions. For the second question, I'm thinking of Jonah, but it's fine if your group members reference other stories from the Old Testament as well.

4. **Discussion** (20 minutes): Invite your group members to share what they wrote down in answer to Let's Talk 4.

5. **Creative Exercise- "Letters in Christ"** (30 minutes): Each person will hopefully have written a letter to himself or herself from God, incorporating verses from Scripture to stay on track with the actual words and character of God. Before having them read their letters, take out an umbrella and open it. While standing under it, explain again the concept of being "in Christ," as I wrote in this session.

   Now, turn in your book to the letter you wrote to yourself from God and read it aloud while standing under the umbrella. Invite each group member to take the umbrella and do the same. If certain individuals are uncomfortable doing this, you can adjust by allowing them to sit while holding the umbrella over them (instead of standing), and/or inviting a different person to read the letter aloud (instead of the person who wrote it).

6. **Talk to God** (10 minutes): As you get to know your group dynamics, you will begin to see how people are comfortable or uncomfortable with praying. Being sensitive to these dynamics, plan your prayer time accordingly. Ideas for topics of prayer are listed at the end of Session Two. Feel free to revise them or add your own.

For next week: Remind participants to read Session Three, to write down their thoughts in the spaces provided, and come prepared to discuss the concepts.

SESSION THREE: Your Communication Style (120 minutes)

1. **Welcome, check-in, and opening prayer** (10 minutes): Welcome your group members. Ask them each to share one word that describes how they are feeling right now. Try to keep this time brief. Pray before you move into discussion of Session Three in your books.

2. **Discussion** (45 minutes): Spend the majority of this time discussing their results from the two-part Communication Style Assessment. Allow each group member to share his or her animal diagram with the abbreviations for their various relationships on it and help them find patterns in the way they communicate.

3. **Creative Exercise- "The Chair"** (15 minutes): Place a chair in the middle of your group and invite one person to sit in it. Ask group members to try different methods of persuasion to try to take the person's place in the chair. Invite others to describe the different methods people use to try to identify how we attempt to get what we want. Set a boundary to protect the person in the chair from anything that could be actually hurtful, such as physical force. To debrief this exercise, discuss Let's Talk 6.

4. **Words from the Word** (40 minutes): Read John 10:27-30 and discuss Question #1, then read Eph. 4:11-16, and discuss Questions 2-4.

5. **Talk to God** (10 minutes): Use the suggestions provided (along with your own topics) to pray as a group. If there are particular group members with difficult conversations coming up this week, pray specifically for those interactions.

For next week: Remind participants to read Session Four, to write down their thoughts in the spaces provided, and come prepared to discuss the concepts.

SESSION FOUR: The Turtle (120 minutes)

1. **Welcome, check-in, and opening prayer** (10 minutes): Welcome your group members. Ask them each to share one concept that God seems to be teaching them already through this study. Pray before you begin discussing the content of Session Four.

2. **Discussion** (45 minutes): Choose a few questions to discuss from Let's Talk 1-6. You will not have time to discuss them all, but be sure to discuss the results from the Turtle Quiz.

3. **Words from the Word** (40 minutes): Ask for a volunteer to recap Exodus 3-4:17. Then discuss Questions 1-2. Ask for a volunteer to read out loud Exodus 32:21-26. Then discuss Questions 3-4, along with Let's Talk 7.

4. **Creative Exercise- "The Pledge"** (2 minutes): For this exercise, invite any willing participants to stand, put their hand on their hearts, and recite "The Turtle Pledge." You read one line or phrase and they repeat it after you.

    "Do-over" (13 minutes): An additional creative option is to allow any group members to "re-do" any conversations they have had in the past in which they did not speak the truth of what they were really thinking or feeling. The group member chooses another member to play the role of the other person and then the duo recreates the scene in which the Turtle was initially silent. This time, however, with newfound courage, the Turtle is able to communicate freely like an Eagle by speaking the truth in love.

5. **Talk to God** (10 minutes): Consider changing up your prayer time this week by pairing your group members. Invite them to use the suggestions provided at the end of the session (along with your own topics) to pray for

205

each other. If there are particular group members, especially Turtles, with difficult conversations coming up this week, remind your group members to pray (and be praying during the week) specifically for those interactions. You may also want to consider other means of support during the week, such as assigning prayer partners or creating a group text thread for people to post requests and praises regarding their interactions.

For next week: Remind participants to read Session Five, to write down their thoughts in the spaces provided, and come prepared to discuss the concepts.

SESSION FIVE: The Fox (120 minutes)

1. **Welcome, check-in, and opening prayer** (10 minutes): Welcome your group members. Ask them to share a moment from the past week in which they experienced faith or fear motivating their communication. Try to keep this sharing brief. Pray before you begin discussing the content of Session Five.

2. **Discussion** (45 minutes): Choose a few questions to discuss from Let's Talk 1-6. You might not have time to discuss them all, but be sure to discuss the results from the Fox Quiz.

3. **Words from the Word** (30 minutes): Ask for volunteers to read any verses in the first 4 chapters of

Jonah that reveal his passive-aggressive tendencies. Talk through questions 1-4.

4. **Creative Exercise- "A Picture of Gifts"** (25 minutes): Ask the group members what gifts they would specifically need to be able to communicate in a challenging relationship life-giving ways (i.e. courage, faith, empathy, trust, surrender, etc.). Invite one willing person to stand in front or in the middle of the others. Then, invite others to "become" different gifts by posturing themselves in a frozen position around her or him. For example, "Courage" might hold up the person's arm. "Peace" might take a position next to the person, as if whispering "Peace, be still," or might be a dove perched close by. "Faith" might kneel in front of the person, facing out and looking up to God, or might be the winds of faith blowing on the person (remember, this is a frozen posture, so the participant will not actually be blowing, but instead will look as if he or she is blowing). Give them the freedom to stand on chairs to create different levels above and around the person. As members take positions, instruct them to say what they represent. Members should stay in place as each new member adds a new posture.

After the frozen portrait is created, take a photo quickly and unobtrusively to send to the person later. Then, instruct the group to make it a moving picture for 15-30 seconds. Say, ready, "Action!" Members can then add motion and sound to their postures, naming the gift they represent ("Courage" might move the arm repetitively, saying, "Courage." "Peace" could actually whisper the word "Peace," etc.). As the 15 seconds comes to an end, advise the person to take in these gifts that only God can give, and then name them again (i.e. courage, faith, etc.). Say, "And, let's end slowly in 5-4-3-2-1." Thank the participants and the person of focus. Invite them to sit down and help them to debrief what they experienced.

If you have time, another group member can be the focus while others create a portrait around him or her.

5. **Talk to God** (10 minutes): Invite participants to stay seated with their palms up, asking God silently to give them His good gifts of freedom, grace, courage, faith, peace, etc. Then, invite them to silently ask God to fill them with His Spirit, to be life-giving communicators through His strength for His kingdom and His glory.

For next week: Remind participants to read Session Seven, to write down their thoughts in the spaces provided in any "Let's Talk" sections, and come prepared to discuss the concepts.

SESSION SIX: The Bulldog (120 minutes)

1. **Welcome, check-in, and opening prayer** (10 minutes): Welcome your group members. Ask them share an element in communication that they believe strongly affects their ability to trust another person (i.e. feeling heard, eye contact, undivided attention, curious questions, history, etc). Try to keep this sharing brief. Pray before you begin discussing the content of Session Six.

2. **Discussion** (45 minutes): Choose a few questions to discuss from Let's Talk 1-7. You probably won't have time to discuss them all, but be sure to discuss the results from the Bulldog Quiz.

3. **Words from the Word** (30 minutes): Ask for volunteers to read aloud Mark 8:32 and Mark 9:5, then discuss the questions. Next, ask for a volunteer to read aloud what he or she thinks are the most courageous verses from Acts 2:1-41. Then discuss the questions. Now, invite a group member to read aloud the paragraph that begins with "Like Peter..." And finally, spend a few minutes discussing Let's Talk 8.

4. **Creative Exercise- "Outside/Inside"** (25 minutes): In this exercise, we will work on developing and communicating trust through vulnerability. To begin, invite one participant to stand and create a pose that represents the tough exterior of a Bulldog, in his or her imagination. Now, invite a second person to stand and create a pose that represents how he or she feels when communicating with a Bulldog. Other Bulldogs might match the aggression, Turtles may hide their heads, and Foxes may take on a sly pose, trying to figure out how to outsmart the Bulldog.

Now, invite the first person to slowly transform his or her pose to represent how a Bulldog might actually feel on the inside. Not the tough exterior, but the soft interior. Then, invite the second person to slowly change his or her pose to connect from a place of vulnerability and trust with the other.

For some, this exercise may be a trigger, bringing up deep emotions based on past interactions and relationships. Use this as a healing time, asking sensitive, curious questions to allow the participants to process any emotions that may bubble up to the surface.

5. **Talk to God** (10 minutes): Spend time praying for the issues that were brought up during your time together. Invite any participants to pray out loud (or silently) a short prayer based on one of the suggestions at the end of this session. Pray specifically for any difficult conversations that participants anticipate this week.

For next week: Remind participants to read Session Six, to write down their thoughts in the spaces provided in any "Let's Talk" sections, and come prepared to discuss the concepts.

SESSION SEVEN: The Eagle (120 minutes)

1. **Welcome, check-in, and opening prayer** (10 minutes): Welcome your group members. Ask what is their greatest challenge to communicating well today. Try to keep this sharing brief. Pray before you begin discussing the content of Session Seven.

2. **Discussion** (45 minutes): Choose a few questions to discuss from Let's Talk 1-8. You probably won't have

time to discuss them all, but be sure to discuss the results from the Eagle Quiz.

3. **Words from the Word** (30 minutes): Ask for volunteers to read aloud the verses associated with each question. Discuss how Jesus chose to communicate differently in different situations. Invite your group members to share verses they found that highlight Jesus' empathy and to discuss how Jesus was forward-thinking.

4. **Creative Exercise- "Soaring Eagle"** (25 minutes): Invite each participant to share his or her drawing with the rest of the group. Encourage group members to ask curious questions to help draw out the person sharing.

5. **Talk to God** (10 minutes): Invite your group members to take a position of humility as they pray. Allow them to pray silently, then you close your time with a prayer aloud.

For next week: Remind participants to read the last session-Session Eight! -to write down their thoughts in the spaces provided in any "Let's Talk" sections, and come prepared to discuss the concepts.

SESSION EIGHT: SOAR (120 minutes)

Note: The Creative Exercise in this session requires a freezer stick or plastic ice cube for each person in your group. You'll also want to bring an insulated lunchbox or cooler to keep them cold. Another option would be to use warm stones. One group leader purchased small stones with scriptures printed on them, warmed them with hand warmers in a small container before and during the small group session, and then afterwards gave each group member a stone to remember the experience. (For hygienic reasons, use a different freezer stick or warm stone for each person.)

1. **Welcome, check-in, and opening prayer** (10 minutes): Welcome your group members. Ask if anyone had the opportunity to speak Eagle this week. Try to keep this sharing brief. Pray before you begin discussing Session Eight.

2. **Discussion** (45 minutes): Discuss what each member wrote down in answer to the questions in Let's Talk 1-5. Keep your discussion moving.

3. **Words from the Word** (25 minutes): Invite a group member to read Isaiah 6:1-8 from the NIV out loud. Discuss participant's answers to questions 1-6.

4. **Creative Exercise** (35 minutes): "Anointed Communication." This final exercise will be worshipful and meaningful. Explain to your group that they are going to experience this passage in Isaiah in a new way. Also explain that at one point you are going to touch their lips with a clean, plastic ice cube, and

that you will use a different one for each person. Invite them to let go and just experience it.

First, start instrumental music playing softly in the background. Now, ask your group members to pray, thanking God for His character and how He has revealed Himself to them during this study. They can pray out loud if they are comfortable. Next, invite your whole group to keep their eyes closed and repeat the following verse after you. (They'll actually repeat it three times so it will soak in well. Try saying it very slowly on the third time.)

LEADER: Repeat after me. "Holy, holy, holy is the LORD Almighty. The whole earth is full of His glory."

GROUP: "Holy, holy, holy is the LORD Almighty. The whole earth is full of His glory."

LEADER: "Holy, holy, holy is the LORD Almighty. The whole earth is full of His glory."

GROUP: "Holy, holy, holy is the LORD Almighty. The whole earth is full of His glory."

LEADER: "Holy, holy, holy is the LORD Almighty. The whole earth is full of His glory."

GROUP: "Holy, holy, holy is the LORD Almighty. The whole earth is full of His glory."

(This next section is to be experienced by each individual. Remind your group to keep their eyes closed. Select one group

member to repeat the following verses after you, keeping his or her eyes closed. For women, consider changing the pronoun to "woman" so that the participant can internalize the concepts more fully.)

LEADER: ___(*Name*)____, repeat after me: "I am a (wo)man of unclean lips."

GROUP MEMBER: "I am a (wo)man of unclean lips."

LEADER: "And I live among a people of unclean lips."

GROUP MEMBER: "And I live among a people of unclean lips."

LEADER: "For my eyes have seen the King, the LORD Almighty."

GROUP MEMBER: "For my eyes have seen the King, the LORD Almighty."

(Now, touch the person's lips for 3 seconds with the cold or warm item.)

LEADER: See, __(Name)___, "this has touched your lips; your guilt is taken away and your sin atoned for." Because of the blood of Jesus, you are forgiven.

(If you are using a warm stone purchased for the participant to keep, you can place it in his or her hands at this point in the exercise.)

(to GROUP) Now, everyone but ____(Name)____, repeat after me: "Whom shall I send, and who will go for us?"

GROUP: Whom shall I send, and who will go for us?

LEADER: __(Name)___, how do you respond?

GROUP MEMBER: "Here I am, send me."

(*Repeat this exercise until each person has experienced it.*)

5. **Talk to God** (10 minutes): As you end the creative exercise, move seamlessly into your prayer time, closing your session by thanking God for your group members, for His calling on your lives, for upcoming difficult conversations, and for the faith and courage to SOAR. Finally, believe God in what He can do in each of you and through you in the future.

References

SESSION ONE

1. James C. McCroskey, "Oral Communication Apprehension," *Human Communication Research* 4, no. 1 (Sept 1977): 78-96.

SESSION TWO

1. Douglas Stone and Bruce. *Difficult Conversations* (New York: Viking, 1999), xxvii.
2. See www.VitalSmarts.com.
3. Brown, Brene. *Daring Greatly* (New York: Gotham Books, 2012) 6.
4. For more on this concept, see Rick Warren, "Faith Is God's Antidote To Fear." Our Daily Hope With Rick Warren. May 21, 2014. http://rickwarren.org/devotional/ english/ faith-is-god's-antidote-to-fear
5. Curt Thompson, *Anatomy of the Soul* (Carol Stream, IL: SaltRiver, 2010) 184-185.
6. Francine Rivers, *The Last Sin Eater* (Carol Stream, IL: Tyndale, 1998).
7. Stone, *Difficult Conversations.*
8. Kerry Patterson, Joseph Grenny, Ron McMillan, Al Switzler, *Crucial Conversations* (New York: McGraw-Hill, 2002).
9. Blackaby, Henry, and Claude King. *Experiencing God* (Nashville: Broadman & Holman, 1994) 15.
10. See www.HeartPerceptionProject.com.
11. Schultze, Quentin. *Communicating for Life* (Grand Rapids, MI: Baker, 2000) 165.

SESSION THREE

1. For more on Myers-Briggs psychological types, see www.MyersBriggs.org.
2. Bobb Biehl, *Why You Do What You Do* (Nashville: Thomas Nelson, 1993) 95.
3. Thompson, *Anatomy of the Soul*, 109-110.
4. Goleman, Daniel. "The Experience of Touch: Research Points to a Critical Role." *The New York Times.* Feb. 2, 1988. http://www.nytimes.com/1988/02/02/science/ the-experience-of-touch-research-points-to-a-critical- role.html.
5. Sue Johnson, *Hold Me Tight* (New York: Little, Brown and Co., 2008), 36.
6. Jill Baird, *Broken and Beloved.* See www.brokenandbeloved.org.
7. INSERM, "New Neuronal Circuits Which Control Fear Have Been Identified," *Science Daily*, November 11, 2010. https://www.sciencedaily.com/releases/2010/11/10 1110131204.htm.

SESSION FOUR

1. Henry Cloud and John Townsend, *Boundaries* (Grand Rapids, MI: Zondervan, 1992), 52.
2. Melody Beattie, *Codependent No More* (Center City, MN: Hazelden, 1986).
3. See Cindy Laverty, "Stuffing Your Feelings," Agingcare.com. August 17, 2015. https://www.agingcare.com/Articles/ignoring-feelings-unhealthy-coping-mechanism-154343.htm.
4. Donald Miller, *Scary Close* (Nashville: Thomas Nelson, 2015), 125.
5. Neil H. Williams, *Gospel Transformation* (Jenkintown, PA: World Harvest Mission, 2006).

SESSION FIVE

1. Melissa Dittmann, "Anger Across the Gender Divide," *American Psychological Association* 34, no. 1 (March 2003): 52.

2. Susan Scutti, "Why Are Women Passive Aggressive?" *Medical Daily*, Oct. 28, 2013. http://www.medical daily.com/why-are-women-passive-aggressive-study-suggests-it-might-be-avoid-physical-harm-261128.

3. Daniel K. Hall-Flavin, "What is passive-aggressive behavior? What are some of the signs?" Mayo Clinic, *Adult Health*, June 9, 2016. http://www.mayoclinic.org/healthy-lifestyle/adult-health/expert-answers/passive-aggressive-behavior/faq-20057901.

4. John Piper. "What Does it Mean for Jesus to Despise Shame?" *Desiring God,* March 29, 2013. http://www.desiringgod.org/articles/what-does-it-mean-for-jesus-to-despise-shame.

SESSION SIX

1. Jon Bastian, "The History of Bulldogs," *Cesar's Way.* https://www.cesarsway.com/about-dogs/breeds/the-history-of-bulldogs.

2. Marion F. Sturkey, "Warrior Culture of the U.S. Marines," *USMC Heritage Press Intl,* 2001. http://www.usmcpress.com/ heritage/marine_corps_mascot.htm.

3. Sylvia Ann Hewlett, *Executive Presence* (New York: Harper Collins, 2014):61.

4. See http://www.bulldoglaw.com/bulldog-law/.

5. John B. Simpson. "Lawyers as Dogs: Bulldogs." *Martin Wren, P.C.,* April 28, 2011. http://martinwrenlaw.com/blog/2011/want-a-bulldog-for-a-lawyer-some-things-to-consider/.

6. "Direct Communication vs. Indirect Communication," *Watershed Associates.* https://www.watershedassociates.com/learning-center-item/direct-communication-vs-indirect-communication.html.

7. Rebecca Bernstein, "7 Cultural Differences in Nonverbal Communication," *Point Park University Online*, March 28, 2017. http://online.pointpark.edu/business/cultural-differences-in-nonverbal-communication/.

8. "The Changing Face of Indian Work Culture," *The Hindu Business Line*, Sept. 10, 2007. http://www.thehindubusinessline.com/todays-paper/tp-opinion/the-changing-face-of-indian-work-culture/article1668907.ece

9. Virginia E. Schein, "The Relationship Between Sex Role Stereotypes and Requisite Management Characteristics," *Journal of Applied Psychology* 57 (1973): 95-100.

10. Hewlett, *Executive Presence.*

11. John Suler, "The Online Disinhibition Effect," *CyberPsychology and Behavior* 7(2004): 321-326.

SESSION SEVEN

1. See http://www.amp.livescience.com.

2. Patricia Edmonds, "For Amorous Bald Eagles, a Death Spiral is a Hot Time," *National Geographic*, July 2016. https://www.nationalgeographic.com/magazine/2016/07/basic-instincts-bald-eagle-mating-dance/.

3. Williams, *Gospel Transformation*, 15.

4. See http://www.defenders.org.
5. Dan Allender and Tremper Longman III, *Bold Love*, (Colorado Springs: NavPress, 1992) 168.
6. English, Tammy and Laura L. Carstensen. "Emotional Experience in the Mornings and the Evenings," *Frontiers in Psychology*, March 6, 2014.
7. Allender and Longman, *Bold Love*, 154-55.
8. Mike Odiegwu, "Defence Spokesman: We'll Not Reveal Whereabouts of Other Chibok Girls," *The Nation*, January 6, 2017. http://thenationonlineng.net/ defence-spokesman-well-not-reveal-whereabouts-chibok-girls/.
9. See Psych Web http://www.psywww.com/intropsych/ ch13_therapies/ assertiveness_training.html
10. Foster Cline and Jim Fay, Parenting with Love and Logic (Colorado Springs: NavPress, 2006) 59.
11. Kenneth Burke, *A Rhetoric of Motives* (Oakland: U of CA Press, 1969), 21.
12. Thompson, *Anatomy of the Soul*, 102.
13. "Farewell to Shadowlands" is the title C.S. Lewis gave to the final chapter in his last book in the Chronicles of Narnia, *The Last Battle* (HarperCollins: New York, 1956). Lewis writes, "There was a real railway accident," said Aslan softly. "Your father and mother and all of you are–as you used to call it in the Shadowlands–dead. The term is over: the holidays have begun. The dream is ended: this is the morning" (228).

SESSION EIGHT

1. Caesar Kalinowski, *The Gospel Primer* (Missio Publishing, 2013). Also see https://www.caesarkalinowski.com/your-story-gods-story/

2. See https://www.scienceofpeople.com/the-science-of-storytelling/.

3. Thompson, *Anatomy of the Soul*, 102.

4. Thierry Steimer, "The Biology of Fear- and anxiety-related] behaviors," *Dialogues in Clinical Neuroscience 4, no. 3* (2002), 231-249

5. *The Holy Bible*, New International Version. Grand Rapids: Zondervan, 1984.

6. Strong's #40: hagios," *Bible Tools: Greek/Hebrew Definitions*. https://www.bibletools.org/index.cfm/fuseaction/Lexicon.show/ID/G40/hagios.htm

Acknowledgements

Heartfelt thanks to…

my clients, students, and friends who bravely told me their communication stories over the past three years. I am forever indebted to you.

Jill, for your encouragement, scientific brilliance, and advice. Strateagles everywhere thank you.

Kellie, my Heart Perception Project partner, for teaching me much about open-heartedness, empathy, and leaning in.

Alice, Allyson, Jesi, Shane, Christina, Kristin, Paige, Elisabeth, Mandy, and the leadership groups at Fellowship Bible Church for embracing this material and giving me helpful feedback.

My Pretty in Ink compadres- Kim, Martha, Jess, Sandy, Marisa, Chris, and Anna for fueling my dreams and offering warm guidance.

David Seibert of Clear Day Media Group for your helpful feedback and positive energy towards promoting the initial ideas in this project.

Joy, Lindsay, Karin, Michalle, Nicky, and Fran, who have prayed for me and been my sounding board.

My father, Steve, and my in-laws, George and Nancy for being my biggest fans and prayer warriors.

My sister, Kimberly, for your sparkly inspiration, your faithful love, and your encouragement to keep writing.

My four boys, Josiah, Jonathan, Joshua, and Justin for keeping me laughing (and reminding me to "Speak Eagle," especially when I'm mad).

My husband, Brian, for helping me hone these ideas, for enduring hours of communication theory-talk, and for being a daily example of an Eagle. (You do waaay more than Jack.)

Finally, to God for being the first and ultimate life-giving Communicator.

11297206R00124

Made in the USA
San Bernardino, CA
03 December 2018